PENGUIN BOOKS

Dare to Be Square

Chris Gilson is a partner in Beber Silverstein & Partners,
an advertising agency with offices in New York, Washington, and Miami. He is the author of college textbooks on
advertising and consumer behavior, and was recently selected by *Advertising Age* as one of the "100 Best and Bright-
est Advertising People in the U.S."

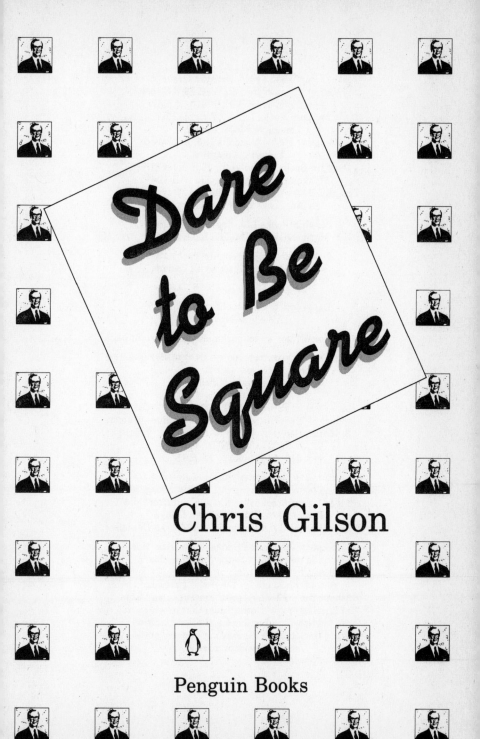

Dare to Be Square

Chris Gilson

Penguin Books

PENGUIN BOOKS
Published by the Penguin Group
Viking Penguin Inc., 40 West 23rd Street,
New York, New York 10010, U.S.A.
Penguin Books Ltd, 27 Wrights Lane,
London W8 5TZ, England
Penguin Books Australia Ltd, Ringwood,
Victoria, Australia
Penguin Books Canada Ltd, 2801 John Street,
Markham, Ontario, Canada L3R 1B4
Penguin Books (N.Z.) Ltd, 182–190 Wairau Road,
Auckland 10, New Zealand

Penguin Books Ltd, Registered Offices:
Harmondsworth, Middlesex, England

First published in Penguin Books 1988
Published simultaneously in Canada

1 3 5 7 9 10 8 6 4 2

Page 262 constitutes an extension of this copyright page.

LIBRARY OF CONGRESS CATALOGING IN PUBLICATION DATA
Gilson, Chris.
Dare to be square / Chris Gilson.
p.   cm.
ISBN 0 14 01.1112 3
1. Conduct of life—Humor.   2. Responsibility—Humor.
3. Maturation (Psychology)—Humor.   I. Title.
PN6231.C6142G55   1988
818'.5402—dc19   88-5918

Printed in the United States of America by
R. R. Donnelley & Sons Company, Harrisonburg, Virginia
Set in Century Schoolbook and Kaufmann Bold
Designed by Beth Tondreau Design
Illustrations by Jennifer Davis and Melissa Daniels

To my Father
The First Debonair Square.

■

And my Mother,
with thanks for the memories.

■

■

AND TO THOSE WHO DARED

Joy and Christopher
Bob Tabian and Maura Lynch,
    ICM's Square Division
Gerry Howard,
    Crusading Editor
Sue Barton
Jennifer Davis
Melissa Daniels
Betty Gayle
Barbara McCrea
Valerie Wells
Joyce Beber
Elaine Silverstein
Myer Berlow
Bob and Susan Bishopric
Paul and Debbie Donnelly
Chas Conklin
Joe Zubi
Hank Goldberg
Gene Powers
Diana Pearson
JoAnn Lederman

Bonnie Blaire
Brenda Rudy
Sydney Barrows
Carol DeLess
Estelle Lee
Jack and Beryl Echlin
Shannon, Johnny and
    Alison Colla
Randy Fisher
Jim and Jackie Copacino
Jerry Rubin
Erika Kovalik
Rick Schmidt
Kevin Hardie
Bill Boxell
Benjamin Davol
Harvey White
Terri Crosby
Bruce Shostak
Dick May
Mel Maguire

CONTENTS

■ ■ ■ ■ ■

one

𝒯HE 𝒮QUARE 𝒟EAL:
Stop All This Nonsense and You Can Join the New Establishment

■ ■ ■ ■ ■ ■

In this chapter you will learn:

■ whether you have a conscience.

■ why you feel hollow in your Reeboks, and guilty for eating the Früsen Glädjé.

■ how to take your rightful place in the New Establishment.

■ how to tell the authentic New Establishment, which will make you feel you've finally come home, from the glitzy Pseudo Establishment, which will make you feel even worse than you do now.

*T*ake off that Sony Walkman, please. Now, let's have a good, solid chat about your life.

Face it. Hip hedonism is dead. Closed down for the foreseeable future by A.I.D.S., M.A.D.D., the S.E.C., and the crash of '87.

Besides, all the parallel bars, Dove Bars, and singles bars in the world haven't made you as happy as you thought they would, have they?

And those fond insider-trading fantasies to the contrary, the odds are that you won't make your fortune overnight in the 1990s unless you marry it or inherit it.

What's left? The good stuff. What's old is what's new. Traditional values. Hardships that build character. Adult wisdom. Acquired wit. Then, when you've paid your dues, a place in the Establishment with its showering of perks and privileges for responsible adults only.

Even if you currently inhabit the hip ozone of *nouvelle cuisine*, Avias, and David Letterman, you may be squarer at the core than you think.

Dare you find out?

■ ■ ■ ■ ■ ■

20 Questions: The Last Self-Test You'll Ever Feel the Need to Take

Just Who Are You?

I don't have a problem that:
1. money, fame, and cosmetic surgery wouldn't solve.
2. keeps me from donating blood.

I expect to find true happiness when:
1. my real life begins.
2. the zinnias come up just perfect next year.

I think it's more important to:
1. teach entrepreneurship in college.
2. teach ethics in kindergarten.

I get most angry at:
1. my credit-stealing blowhole of a boss.
2. families who start whispering in church.

I'd say one thing I don't worry much about is:
1. other people's problems.
2. the Beastie Boys showing up unexpectedly for dinner.

Spiritual Needs

I did est and:
1. still think Werner is God.
2. only felt good at the bathroom breaks.

I sat in the mud baths at Esalen and:
1. felt totally centered.
2. got filthy dirty.

I tried primal scream and:
1. let go of my anger.
2. hated raising my voice.

I experienced Rolfing and I'm:
1. free of a childhood trauma.
2. glad they only did it to the cat.

I have been in therapy for only:
1. eleven years.
2. a dislocated thumb.

Square Dreams: "When will my real life begin?"

THE ULTIMATE TEST: SEEING YOURSELF IN A NORMAN ROCKWELL

Go ahead. You can handle it. Gaze into those noble faces. See common folk uplifting themselves through the squarest of pursuits.

The travelers who say grace in a diner, oblivious to the seedy world around them. First you might feel a kind of embarrassment. Then maybe a vague yearning . . . where *are* those people today?

The citizen who speaks up at the town meeting. Naïve clod, or could he know something about American core values that you don't?

The gawky teenagers at the soda fountain. Too uncool for any school you know. But they got along without a stretch limo to their prom. And they probably aren't using the 800-Cocaine hotline today, either.

Now let's turn to the unkempt modern dad, slithering down into his oh-so-modern chair, too caught up in low-rent hedonism to join his family at church. Smoking! Unshaven! In his bathrobe after 10 A.M.! Feeling good about yourself, Dad?

If you think everyone but Dad looks happier than you are, you're right. *Moral:* The more you look and act like a Norman Rockwell character, the better you're going to feel.

Before you lapse into a hopeless "I'll never be square" depression, a word to the wise: Perfectly square contentment can be achieved through a little hard work and a lot of gumption!

Even if you stand before your mirror a fully grown adult, hair spiked with mousse to resemble a porcupine's back, and shoulders padded like an aircraft carrier deck, you can still be one of us.

Adulthood need not be the confusing, frustrating, and unsatisfying state where you reside.

Look at the adults of the 1950s. They built character by surviving the Great Depression and its economic correction known as World War II, that last epic struggle between pure Good and goose-stepping, death's-head Evil, so they could relax and enjoy their material rewards. Raise the tail fin on that '59 Caddy, and stick a set of rocket lights in! Let's add a bigger freezer section to that Kelvinator, to make more room for frozen dinners and less work for Mom! Where their adult choices were simple (Ford or Chevy, Coke or Pepsi, Republican or Pinko), yours seem mottled with doubts and fears.

Steeled by no personal hardships greater than a dead weight that sprains your wrist or food processors that fail to slice the carrots correctly, you feel guilty for enjoying affluence without its necessary correlative: mighty personal sacrifice. What you do not suffer enough to achieve offers too little reward.

Driven by no greater goals than your own selfish ambitions, you flail out at random for meaning in your shallow life. Shall I marry? Have children? Buy zero coupon bonds? A fur-lined raincoat? "Where's the beef?" wasn't just the theme of a Wendy's commercial, but the humanist's wailing discovery of the Great Aching Void inside the modern soul!

Armed by no abiding values other than the current wisdom on "Nightline," it's no wonder that you feel crushed by the pressures of the world around you, defeated by wilier competitors at work, betrayed by authority when your German-built car lurches out of control and slams into your mailbox.

But all that can be put behind you now, and you *can* go home again. First we will see where America lost its way, and you with it. Then we will swiftly and surely banish the forces of uncertainty raging in your breast and make you spiritually whole.

OUR SQUARE ROOTS

Perhaps you'll recall that we once had a "Protestant Ethic" in this country. Work hard. Do for others. Virtue is its own reward. This became increasingly unpopular as great modern philosophers such as P. T. Barnum and Jerry Rubin decided that narcissism and self-hype would serve us better.

The Protestant Ethic may be traced directly to the American Puritans. Thus it was easily branded as unfun by hip modernists. Puritans, they said, were zealots who burned women at the stake for the sort of cranky behavior we freely tolerate in bank tellers and prevented colonial Hugh Hefners from fulfilling their destinies.

In fact, the Puritans created the first square Nirvana: the original Eastern Establishment. They were industrious. They got along together. They cared for their poor and helpless and, in their spare time, founded both Harvard and Yale.

And their sturdy ethic of industry, authority, and light-to-moderate hypocrisy kept America thriving for the first three hundred years.

▪ ▪ ▪ ▪ ▪ ▪

Square Roots:
Life in the Puritan Village

Salem, Massachusetts, c. 1690

Religion
Puritan villagers disliked pulpit-thumping displays of Fundamentalism, preferring the more intellectual nature of Calvinism.

Trades and Professions
Puritan villagers busied themselves developing land, farming, and followed the professions of divine (churchman), soldier, and physician.

Entertainment
Puritan children played with simple, handcrafted toys and dolls.

Adults drank at ordinations, smoked tobacco pipes, played cards, and discussed religious trivia.

Education
Puritan schools were strict, challenging, and the successful went on to either Yale or Harvard.

Sport
Puritan villagers actively engaged in witch-hunting and displayed captured witches publicly.

Sex
Puritan teenagers could enjoy the approved practice of "bundling," which permitted them to lie together to keep warm, separated only by blankets sewed down the middle between them. Or, if lucky, by a simple board called the bundling board.

▪ ▪ ▪ ▪ ▪ ▪

LOST IN INNER SPACE

Then came the sixties, and the rest is shameful history.

Nobody wanted to work anymore. Postmen stole your mail so they wouldn't have to deliver it. Auto workers left Coke bottles rattling in the door of your new Mustang. Supreme Court Justices grew sideburns, and let Madelyn Murray ban school prayer.

Back in the sensible forties, Abraham Maslow devised a handy chart for why we behave the way we do. He called it his Needs Hierarchy, and it looked like a triangular ladder with needs to meet from bottom to top.

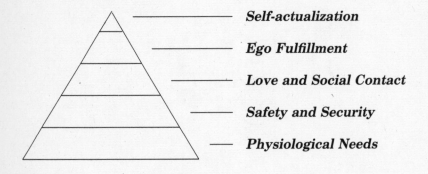

Self-actualization

Ego Fulfillment

Love and Social Contact

Safety and Security

Physiological Needs

How Americans met those needs over the twenty years following 1967's "Summer of Love" reveals where we went wrong. First there was the decade of disco, self-awareness, and silly drinks. Let's call it:

The Harvey Wallbanger Era (1967–1977)

Motto: "Let's talk about me."

Song: "It's My Turn"

Bible: Looking Out for #1
Forget moral absolutes like everyone else and you won't be their doormat anymore.

Spokesperson: Jerry Rubin

Headquarters: Club Med

Moment: White House Chief of Staff Hamilton Jordan spits an Amaretto and Cream into a woman's décolletage at a Georgetown singles bar.

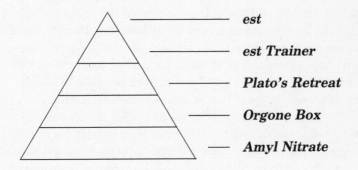

- *est*
- *est Trainer*
- *Plato's Retreat*
- *Orgone Box*
- *Amyl Nitrate*

In the Harvey Wallbanger Era, everyone saw everybody else getting away with something, and dropped whatever they might have been working on at the time to join them.

Americans discovered pocket calculators so they could avoid the mental strain of adding 3 to 11, *People* magazine to parade an endless assortment of fifteen-minute fame seekers sandwiched between the regulars (Liz Taylor, Jackie O-later-K-again, Woody Allen and Diane Keaton, porn star Marilyn Chambers, who epitomized what an Ivory Soap girl grew up to be if she came of age in the seventies), designer jeans worn with high heels, and the costume that expressed the ethos of the era, the incomparable American Leisure Suit.

▪ ▪ ▪ ▪ ▪ ▪

Milestones of the Harvey Wallbanger Era:

7HE ßIRTH OF THE £EISURE ßUIT

In the early 1970s, when everyone had already decided that they preferred leisure to work, a Pasadena, California, salesman named Harold Luck invented the leisure suit.

Late for an evening at the Tele-Date Bar, Harold acted in desperation. He took an unused pair of hedge clippers and hacked the lower third of his jacket lapels from the double-knit polyester suit he had been wearing to his last sales presentation of time-share condos in Tijuana.

To conceal the ragged edges, he pulled the elephantine collar of his boldly striped polyester shirt outside his collar, unbuttoned the top three buttons to expose his graying chest hair and the gold-plated medallion he had been wearing underneath.

Harold was unsure of the reception he would enjoy at the Tele-Date. He settled at his table and waited. The phone rang.

"Hi. I'm at Table 5. What's that you're wearing?"

The following night three of Harold's friends joined him at the Tele-Date, all with their lapels hacked off and with their shirt collars pulled outside.

A menswear buyer for Macy's happened to be sitting at the next table.

"Say, what's that you're wearing?"

"That's his loser suit," Harold's best friend joked.

But the buyer misunderstood and rushed to the phone to launch a forgettable moment in American history.

▪ ▪ ▪ ▪ ▪ ▪

By 1978 the Baby Boomers who were dozing on marijuana during the 1960s and Quaaludes during the early part of the seventies were beginning to feel the hot and furious breath of a new generation closing behind them, then passing them by with a faceful of Mercedes fumes. The Yuppies!

Flinty-eyed twenty-five-year-old couples made $1.8 million a year between them on Wall Street and were so pressed for time that they bounced to the office on $125 jogging shoes. The money was there, what else mattered? Romance became a quaint concept best satirized by Madonna, "Dallas," and "Dynasty." Rich! Dazzling! And you could do it overnight with very little hard work and inside trading!

The Yuppie Era was upon us, ushering in Ronald Reagan and hustling the leisure suits out the back door pronto.

The Yuppie Era (1978–1987)

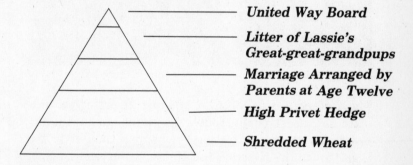

— *United Way Board*

— *Litter of Lassie's Great-great-grandpups*

— *Marriage Arranged by Parents at Age Twelve*

— *High Privet Hedge*

— *Shredded Wheat*

Motto: "Poverty sucks."

Song: "Material Girl"

Bible: Creating Wealth
Step out of the unemployment line and become a real estate mogul via "nothing down" deals.

Spokesman: Dennis Levine

Headquarters: Offshore

Moment: Yuppie cops Sonny Crockett and Ricardo Tubbs tackle undercover work (salary $32,500 a year) with the only white Ferrari Testarossa in downtown Miami (cost $120,000).

▪ ▪ ▪ ▪ ▪ ▪

The First Yuppies:
John and Maureen Dean

The Watergate scandal gave America its prototype, ultimate role model Yuppie couple determined to have it all.

John, a government attorney, became counsel to the President in the Nixon White House at the tender age of thirty-one, drove a Porsche, owned a townhouse, and borrowed Watergate-related cash from his office safe to finance his honeymoon with former flight attendant Maureen.

While his superiors at the White House pressured him to get a proper cover-up together, Dean was negotiating to be star witness for the Senate Investigating Committee on Watergate, implicating President Nixon and company in assorted dirty tricks.

After a brief prison term, John wrote the best-seller *Blind Ambition* with ghostwriter Taylor Branch. Not to be outdone, Maureen set to work on her own book.

John, played by Martin Sheen in the made-for-TV movie *Blind Ambition,* went on to sell radio programming and form his own holding company. But Maureen, today a Hills stockbroker, has clearly pulled ahead in the literary Dean-stakes with her fiction entry *Washington Wives.*

They live happily in Beverly Hills.

■ ■ ■ ■ ■ ■

But what a moral mess the Yuppies made, with their Contragates and offshore scams.

Chief executives stopped running their companies to concentrate on putting together golden parachute deals to make money if their firms were acquired. Sayonara, suckers! I'm off to Bimini in my fifty-eight-foot yacht!

Was there at last no sense of decency left? No fairness? Ha! Then came the New Puritans like a cavalry charge! Dennis Levine in handcuffs! Ivan Boesky off to jail! Adnan Khashoggi's yacht repossessed by creditors! Joe Biden caught giving quotes without benefit of the proper credits!

An old-style witch-hunt, just like Salem!

And not a moment too soon, it's the dawn of:

The Restoration Era! (1987–   )

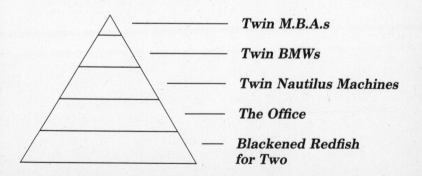

— Twin M.B.A.s

— Twin BMWs

— Twin Nautilus Machines

— The Office

— Blackened Redfish for Two

Motto: "You don't have to memorize the truth."

Song: "The Party's Over"

Bible: *McGuffey's Eclectic Reader*. The American child's primer on personal industry and morality from 1836 to 1920.

Spokesperson: Cotton Mather, 1663–1728. Preacher, author, Harvard man, scientist, and scholar, who articulated the tenets of American Puritanism in Massachusetts.

Headquarters: Home, church, and school.

Moment: Evangelists Jim and Tammy Bakker forced to liquidate, proving that no proper minister would use electronic media.

Square. Safe. Contented. Doing your part for the community. And running things besides!

*W*AGES OF *S*IN:
A *D*ISAPPOINTED *C*OTTON *M*ATHER *C*HIDES THE *M*AYFLOWER *M*ADAM

"It is the true spirit of a gentleman to make his conversation easy to everyone especially to such as Madam . . . (but) every calling whereby none but the lusts of man are nourished should be rejected!"

"But here I was without a standard college education, much less an M.B.A. . . ."

"Should a person of your great esteem and figure prevail to appear as patrons of a work so evidently calculated for the best of them to be erected . . . ?"

"I really love my business. . . . Our clients worked in every business and profession you could imagine . . . including a Catholic priest who liked to smoke marijuana while he burned incense, and an Orthodox rabbi who insisted on wearing his fringed prayer garment to bed."

"My purpose was to have assembled a number of pious gentlemen . . . making prayers on your behalf . . . which I proposed then to have printed with the story of your affair. . . ."

"At that moment, writing a book was the last thing on my mind."

From Kenneth Silverman, ed., *Selected Letters of Cotton Mather* (Baton Rouge, La.: Louisiana State University Press, 1971).

From Sydney Biddle Barrows and William Novak, *The Mayflower Madam* (New York: Ballantine/Ivy, 1987).

■ ■ ■ ■ ■ ■

Oh, what a great time for a human being of goodwill to be alive! What an era for an innocent babe to be born into! What a reaffirmation of the godly spirit! What an occasion to push the outer limits of marital sex!

In fact, let us dream boldly on! What an opportunity to save the Third World through Christianity! What a vast Empire of Truth and Righteousness could be fashioned, under the firm hand of a few enlightened New Establishment leaders and a crusading army of Christian purpose!!

But we digress.

SQUARE HEAVEN:
LIFE IN THE
NEW ESTABLISHMENT

Let's clear up the confusing mess of what Establishment you should be joining.

At a casual glance, it would seem that what were once the privileged few have now become the privileged many. Today there are 1,500,000 millionaires in the United States, most of whom achieved their wealth by living on a piece of California real estate during the seventies.

But make no mistake. These Johnny-and-Jeannie-come-latelies are *not* the New Establishment. The Establishment never changes. Or even twitches. It is unmoved by the rantings of new money stamping its feet at the door for a better table. Unimpressed by the European glitterati stretching their nude, languid bodies on Sardinian beaches, paparazzi in hot pursuit.

The New Establishment still wears glasses with tortoiseshell rims, and vest pocket watches, not gold Rolexes with diamond bezels.

Here is the Established Social Order made simple:

CLASS	BEHAVIOR
1. Old Rich	Hiding
2. New Rich	Flashing
3. Responsible Middle	Doctoring and lawyering
4. Mastercard Middle	Shopping at major malls
5. Lumpen Middle	Shopping at auto parts stores
6. Poor People	Parenting

Money isn't everything. The Establishment also judges people by their values and attitudes. While only a few families have been around long enough to be known as "Good Families," there are opportunities in all rungs leading down the ladder to be considered a "Nice Family."

A Nice Family teaches its children the values of hard work, fair play, devotion to duty, and knows how to behave.

For example, the Windsors of England are a Good Family because they can trace their lineage back to William the Conquerer and possess legitimate old money complete with priceless heirlooms. However, while it would seem that families like the Windsors are born with lifetime membership in the Establishment, remember that behavior counts too. This places the Windsors in current jeopardy through the hip antics of daughter-in-law Diana, who goes to Dire Straits concerts and applies meaningfully negative body language in the presence of her husband, Charles. Therefore, we must qualify the Windsors as holding Good Family status only so long as Diana keeps herself and Charles out of serious marital difficulties.

Now let us consider the case of Jim and Margaret Anderson of Springfield. While Jim is only an insurance salesman, he and Margaret make up in old-fashioned values what they may lack in old (or new) money. Witness the close supervision of their children's behavior, the absence of apparent sexual contact between them, and Jim's good sense in never turning directly to the camera and delivering a sales pitch for his company's whole-life policy.

"Good" and "Nice" Families

	Who	Description
Good	The P.D.* Windsors	A model old-money family, driven by duty.
	*Pre-Diana	

	Who	Description
Nice	The Andersons: Mom, Dad, Betty, Bud, and "Princess"	Recurring issue: resisting influence of the kids' hippier friends.

New Establishment Role Models for Today

In the Restoration Era our behavior will grow up. The much-admired childish traits of the sixties, seventies, and eighties will be found wanting, while the rediscovered value of doing what's right will soar in popular appeal.

Here's how today's sociopathic role models will lose out to shining examples for enlightened Neo-Puritans.

Authority Role Models

OUT: Narcissus

Narcissus, as some of us who bothered to study in school know, was a preening creature of Greek mythology who fell in love with his own reflection. And what a hero he became to the Me Generation!

He was adopted as the dashboard patron saint of every celebrity since Jack Parr told us how *he* really felt (never mind the stupid guests) as host of the old "Tonight Show."

His spirit has been immortalized in ads for Leona Helmsley. In the Nautilus Clubs. And in "Garry Shandling's Show."

IN: **Moses**

Moses could not have labored more diligently to look out for others. He presented us with the Ten Commandments. He led his fellow citizens on the mighty Exodus out of Egypt, renouncing all the blandishments of a corrupt and greedy civilization.

For Moses could have been rich! A pharaoh's adopted son! In the eighties Yuppies scoffed at his altruism. In the nineties he will make a moral comeback.

Old Money Role Models

OUT: **Marie Antoinette**

The ultimate mentor of all American princesses, Marie (known to her subjects as "Madame Deficit") moved her pre–Louis Vuitton luggage into Versailles as a fifteen-year-old with a short attention span and an eye for luxury. She took revenge on her busy husband through shopping sprees that bankrupted the royal treasury and pushed a grumbling peasantry to storm the Bastille, launching the French Revolution.

IN: **Elizabeth I**

A paragon of wisdom and virtue, Elizabeth I practiced frugality, hated corruption. She earned the best credit rating of any European monarch and with clever personal diplomacy kept England out of costly wars during her reign. She cultivated "The Virgin Queen" role as an ongoing negotiation, receiving suitors from all the royal houses of Europe, who could not, of course, go to war with England while pursuing her hand in marriage.

Even when she was bad she was good. Her nastiest trait was suppressing the British Puritan reform movement, which ultimately served us well by forcing Puritans to America.

New Money Role Models

OUT: Peron

Heroine of the pop opera *Evita,* Little Eva's social climbing propelled her from the dusty pampas to rule Argentina with her husband Juan Peron. Thanks to her humble beginnings, Evita could enthrall the simple folk even when wearing Chanel dresses purchased by skimming off the Eva Peron Foundation she established as patronage to the poor.

Evita died at thirty-three. But her continuing spell over Juan drove him to move her carefully preserved cadaver into the Casa Rosada as a third member of Argentina's first family when he assumed the Presidency with his new wife, Isabel.

EVERY GOOD AND EXCELLENT THING
STANDS MOMENT BY MOMENT
ON THE RAZOR'S EDGE OF DANGER
AND MUST BE FOUGHT FOR

IN: **Perot**

H. Ross Perot, a self-made billionaire, built an empire by adopting the role of ultimate corporate father figure. From an office decorated with paintings of American Revolutionary heroes, he masterminded a daring paramilitary plan to rescue a group of his managers held captive in Tehran by revolutionary Iranians months before they seized the American embassy.

Perot left the board of General Motors disgusted by the firm's self-centered management style. He describes his greatest accomplishment as his five children.

Political Conscience Role Models

OUT: **Machiavelli**

Kicked out of office for raising an army against the Medici in Renaissance Italy, Machiavelli skulked into an early retirement and wrote *The Prince,* all about *his* role model, Cesare Borgia. His moral: "The end justifies the means."

Machiavelli's works inspired most government and business leaders of the seventies and eighties, as well as the limited-production Machiavelli automobile—a Pontiac Firebird cosmetically doctored to look like a Ferrari.

IN: **Elliot Richardson**

In 1973 President Nixon appointed Richardson Attorney General during the fast-bubbling Watergate scandal. Then, on October 21, 1973, Nixon demanded that Richardson fire Special Watergate Prosecutor Archibald Cox. Richardson refused and resigned his office in protest, followed the same evening by his Assistant Attorney General William Ruckelshaus; that left Solicitor General Robert Bork to fire Cox on Nixon's order. (The same Robert Bork who expected to become a Supreme Court Justice sporting a billy-goat beard.)

Richardson has never been caught plagiarizing speeches or aboard any charter boat with a name like "Monkey Business."

THE PROTOTYPE ESTABLISHMENT ROLE MODEL: MALE

JOHN PUTNAM THATCHER
Senior Vice President
Sloan Guaranty Trust Company
New York City

Age: About sixty

Birthplace: Sunapee, New Hampshire

Occupation: Banker. Head of Trust Department at "The Sloan,"
an Old Guard Wall Street financial institution.

Avocation: Cooperating with the proper authorities to solve
murders perpetrated on and by the Sloan's clients.

A Snapshot in the Life: ". . . Even John Thatcher had not escaped unscathed from the festive season. . . . Inevitably the set of
in-laws he liked least was centered within easy reach of the city. . . .

"He incautiously opened his visit with an inquiry about his
daughter's health, and Laura, nearing the end of her fourth month
of pregnancy, replied in detail, leaving her father with the gloomy
conviction that her conversation of the last ten years had become
largely obstetrical.

". . . He retreated to the dining room to mix himself a drink, only to be cornered by Mrs. Carlson, who wanted to discuss both her investments and the approach of her latest grandchild. Outraged at the idea of discussing his daughter's Fallopian tubes with anybody, he escaped only to fall prey to a long and ill-informed analysis of the international situation by Cardwell Carlson, a professor of classics at Columbia.

"Release eventually came only with the early morning train to New York. His cup of grievance overflowed when Miss Corsa's absence made it impossible for him to deal with his mail. Quelling the impulse to start ringing up hospitals, he reminded himself that it was the day after Christmas and, just because she never had been late, it was unreasonable to suppose that she couldn't be if she set her mind to it. Thatcher sat and waited, counting the things he couldn't do until she arrived. He succeeded in working himself up into a very satisfying temper by the time Miss Corsa burst in.

" 'That's all right, Miss Corsa,' he snapped, breaking into her flow of apologies, 'but please get Nicolls in here as fast as you can.' His tone implied that the affairs of the Sloan Guaranty Trust had reached a crisis during her unscheduled absence, which only the immediate production of Ken Nicolls could resolve. Rose Corsa, still in her overcoat, flew to the telephone, distressed and guilty but gratified that her presence was indispensable."

From Emma Lathen,
Banking on Death (New York:
Pocket Books, 1983), pp. 35–39.

Accomplishments chronicled in:
John Putnam Thatcher books by Emma Lathen. Recommended reading:

▪ *A Place for Murder*

▪ *Accounting for Murder*

▪ *Murder Against the Grain*

THE PROTOTYPE ESTABLISHMENT ROLE MODEL: FEMALE

EMILY POST (1873–1960)
"The First Lady of Etiquette"

Birthplace: Baltimore, Maryland

Occupation: Author of *Etiquette: The Blue Book of Social Usage* (1922), *How to Behave Though a Debutante* (1928), and *Children Are People* (1940)

On Polite Conversation:

FORBIDDEN GROUND

Avoiding Sore Subjects

> ... *If you care too intensely about a subject, it is dangerous to allow yourself to say anything.*

The Tactless Blunder

> ... *Commonplace examples of tactlessness include such remarks as "Twenty years ago you were the prettiest girl in Philadelphia." Or in the pleasantest tone of voice to a woman whose only son has just married, "Why is it, do you suppose, that young wives always dislike their mothers-in-law?"*
>
> *If you want to be sought after, you must not talk about the unattractiveness of old age to the elderly, about the joys of dancing and skating to the lame, or about the advantages of ancestry to the self-made.*

UNPLEASANT TYPES

The Cutting Wit

> *The man or woman of brilliant wit is in great danger of making enemies. Sharp wit tends to produce a feeling of mistrust even while it stimulates.*

For Those Who Talk Too Much

> *The faults of commission are far more serious than those of omission; there are seldom regrets for what you left unsaid. "Better to keep your mouth closed and be thought a fool than open it and remove all doubt."*

From *Etiquette* (New York: Harper & Row, 1984), pp. 40–43.

■ ■ ■ ■ ■ ■

SQUARE HEAVEN:
LIFE IN THE NEW ESTABLISHMENT VILLAGE

Sharon, Connecticut, c. 1990

Religion

New Establishment villagers dislike pulpit-thumping displays of fundamentalism by TV evangelists, preferring the more intellectual nature of Presbyterian thought.

Trades and Professions

New Establishment villagers busy themselves developing real estate, farming unprofitable cattle for tax shelters, and follow the professions of vicar (churchman), military officer, and physician.

Entertainment

New Establishment children play with simple, handcrafted educational toys and dolls.

Adults drink at the country club, smoke pipes, play bridge, and discuss the questions in *Trivial Pursuits*.

Education

New Establishment preparatory schools are strict, challenging, and the successful students can go on to either Yale or Harvard.

Sport

New Establishment villagers actively engage in duck hunting, and display captured ducks publicly.

Sex

New Establishment teenagers can enjoy the approved practice of co-ed dorms, which permits them to lie together separated only by a Puritanical code of behavior. Or, if lucky, by a small sheepskin known as a "condom."

ONWARD AND UPWARD
BY YOUR OWN BOOTSTRAPS!

If you want true adult happiness, you must learn from the role models for our time.

Stop talking about yourself, and stiffen that upper lip.

Take those silly designer sneakers off your feet and get a sensible pair of brogues.

And if you can't think of something nice to say about someone, don't say anything at all.

Establishment aspirants will now kindly put on a tie or a skirt (never both at the same time), so we may begin to pump up your character with simple exercises and constant repetitions.

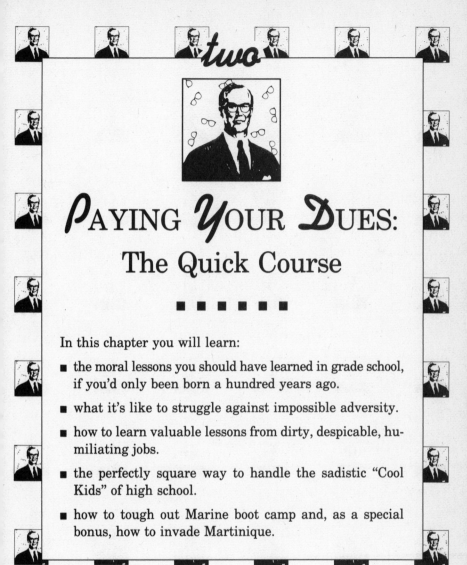

two

*P*AYING *Y*OUR *D*UES:
The Quick Course

■ ■ ■ ■ ■ ■

In this chapter you will learn:

- the moral lessons you should have learned in grade school, if you'd only been born a hundred years ago.

- what it's like to struggle against impossible adversity.

- how to learn valuable lessons from dirty, despicable, humiliating jobs.

- the perfectly square way to handle the sadistic "Cool Kids" of high school.

- how to tough out Marine boot camp and, as a special bonus, how to invade Martinique.

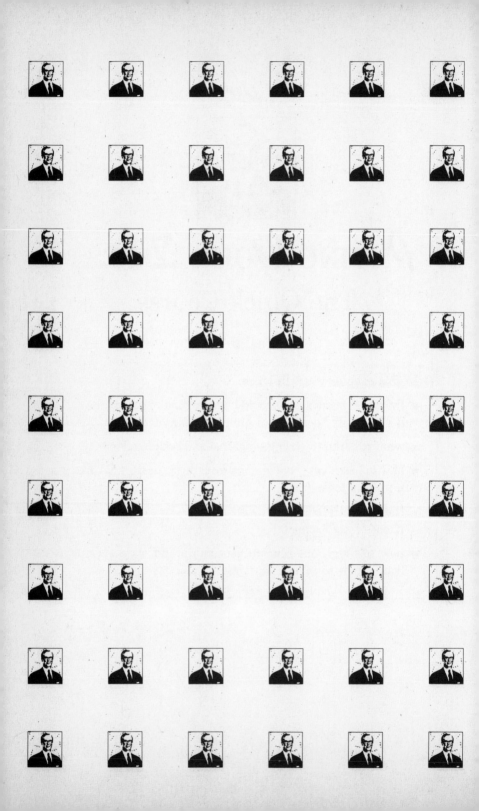

*S*ome of us had to build character the hard way. Others merely bought this book.

Because you have probably devoted your entire childhood and early adult life to the easy, convenient, self-indulgent, and hip, we have no time to waste now on idle chatter. We will need to whip you into man- or womanhood swiftly and surely. Here you will learn the mental and physical lessons you missed in those formative early years spent listening to the Rolling Stones. Or watching Ozzie Osborne bite the heads off bats.

But first you will have to cleanse hedonistic and cynical images from your mind by applying the brainwashing technique known to our Puritan forebears as the Miracle of the Dunking Chair. Then your mind will be fresh and pure to learn the experiences that will give you character.

Re-creating the Miracle of the Dunking Chair at home.

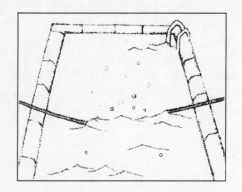

The Formative Years: Five Lessons You Should Have Learned in Grade School

Our lessons for today—I SAID OUR LESSONS FOR TODAY—come from *McGuffey's Fourth Reader*. They are condensed to teach you correct values without time-consuming entertainment value. Listen closely.

I. Consequences of Idleness

1. When he was twelve, George Doner went to an academy to prepare to enter college. His father was at great expense in obtaining books for him, clothing him, and paying his tuition.

2. But George thought of nothing but present pleasure. He would often go to school without having made any preparation for his morning lesson; and, when called to recite with his class, he would stammer and make such blunders that the rest of the class could not help laughing at him.

3. At last George went with his class to enter college. Now came hard times for poor George. In college there is not much mercy shown to bad scholars, and George had neglected his studies so long that now he could not keep up with his class.

4. You would have pitied him if you could have seen him trembling in his seat, every moment expecting to be called upon to recite. Sometimes he would make such ludicrous blunders that the whole class would burst into a laugh. He was wretched, of course. He had been idle so long that he hardly knew how to apply his mind to study. All the good scholars avoided him; they were ashamed to be seen in his company.

5. He left college, despised by everyone. A few months ago I met him, a poor wanderer, without money and without friends. Such are the wages of idleness.

Moral for Today:

College students today create the fiction that they are zoned-out know-nothings only to lure the idle to universities, where they think they will get by with no work. True SAT scores of hard-working students are altered downward by the Educational Testing Service to complete the deception.

Once admitted to college, however, the idle are subjected to punishing peer pressure for their bad study habits, which will ruin their remaining adult lives.

Caught napping in school.

II. True Manliness

1. "Please, Mother, do sit down and let me try my hand," said Fred Liscom, a bright, active boy twelve years old. Mrs. Liscom, looking pale and worn, was moving languidly about, trying to clear away the breakfast she had scarcely tasted.

2. She smiled and said, "You, Fred, you wash dishes?" "Yes, indeed, Mother," replied Fred. "I should be a poor scholar if I couldn't, when I've seen you do it so many times. Just try me."

3. A look of relief came over his mother's face as she seated herself in her low rocking chair. Fred washed the dishes and put them in the closet.

4. Of course he reported this at school, and various were the greetings poor Fred received at recess. "Well, you're a brave one to stay at home washing dishes," his friend Tom Barton said. "Girl boy!" "Pretty Bessie!" "Lost your apron, haven't you, Polly!"

5. Fred was not wanting either in spirit or courage, and he was

strongly tempted to resent these insults and to fight some of his tormentors. But his consciousness of right and his love for his mother helped him.

6. "Fire, fire!" The cry crept out on the still night air, and the fire bells began to ring. Fred was wakened by the alarm and the red light streaming into his room. He dressed himself in a moment, almost, and tapped at the door of his mother's bedroom.

7. Fred found Tom Barton outside his house, in safety. "Where is Katy?" he asked. Tom, trembling with terror, seemed to have had no thought but of his own escape. He said, "Katy is in the house!" "In what room?" asked Fred. "In that one," pointing to a window in the upper story.

8. A ladder was quickly brought and placed against the house. Fred mounted it, dashed in the sash of the window, and pushed his way into the room where the poor child lay nearly suffocated with smoke. He roused her with some difficulty, carried her to the window, and placed her upon the sill. They had scarcely reached the ground before a crash of falling timbers told them that they had barely escaped with their lives.

9. Tom Barton never forgot the lesson of that night, and he came to believe, and to act upon the belief, in after years, that true manliness is in harmony with gentleness, kindness, and self-denial.

Moral for Today:

There is nothing unmanly about a male helping with the dishes. Provided, of course, that he is widely known to have saved a female child from a raging fire.

III. The Noblest Revenge

1. "I will have revenge on him, that I will, and make him heartily repent it," said Philip to himself with a countenance quite red

with anger. His mind was so enraged that he did not see Stephen, who happened at that instant to meet him.

2. "Who is that," said Stephen, "on whom you intend to be revenged?" Philip, as if awakened from a dream, stopped short. "Ah," said he, "you remember my bamboo, a very pretty cane which was given by my father, do you not? Look! There it is in pieces. It was Farmer Robinson's son who reduced it to this worthless state."

3. "To be sure," said Stephen, "he is a very wicked boy, and is already very properly punished for being such. Very unluckily for him, he chanced to see a bee hovering about a flower which he caught, and was going to pull off its wings out of sport, when the animal stung him, and flew away in safety to the hive. The pain put him into a furious passion, and, like you, he vowed revenge. He accordingly procured your stick, and thrust it into the beehive. That is how it was broken.

4. "In an instant the whole swarm flew out, and alighting upon him stung him in a hundred different places. He uttered the most piercing cries and rolled upon the ground in the excess of his agony. His father immediately ran to him, but could not put the bees to flight until they had stung him so severely that he was confined several days to his bed.

5. "Thus, you see, he was not very successful in his pursuit of revenge. I would advise you, therefore, to pass over his insult."

6. A few days afterward, Philip saw this ill-natured boy fall as he was carrying home a heavy log of wood, which he could not lift again. Philip ran to him and helped him to replace it on his shoulder. Young Robinson was quite ashamed at the thought of this unmerited kindness and heartily repented of his behavior. Philip went home quite satisfied. "This," said he, "is the noblest vengeance I could take, in returning good for evil."

Moral for Today:

He who steals a cane is likely to be stung by bees, thus no special strategy for revenge is indicated. Moreover, it will inflict additional guilt on the stung individual if you should help him with a heavy log. Unless, of course, the thief is a sociopath who cannot feel guilt. In such a case, rehabilitation will be doubtful and the death penalty may be desirable.

IV. The Young Witness

1. A little girl nine years of age was brought into court and offered as a witness against a prisoner who was on trial for a crime committed in her father's house.

2. "Did you ever take an oath?" inquired the judge.

3. The little girl stepped back with a look of horror, and the red blood rose and spread in a blush all over her face and neck, as she answered, "No, sir." She thought he intended to ask if she had ever used profane language.

4. "Well," said the judge, "place your hand upon this Bible and listen to what I say," and he repeated slowly and solemnly the following oath: "Do you swear that in the evidence which you shall give in this case you will tell the truth, and nothing but the truth, and that you will ask God to help you?"

5. "I do," she replied.

6. "Has anyone talked with you about being a witness in court here against this man?" inquired the judge.

7. "Yes, sir," she replied, "my mother heard they wanted me to be a witness, and last night she called me to her room and asked me to recite the Ten Commandments, and then we kneeled down together, and she prayed that I might understand how wicked it was to bear false witness against my neighbor, and that God would help me, a little child, to tell the truth as it was before Him."

8. "Do you believe this?" asked the judge, while a tear glistened in his eye, and his lip quivered with emotion.

9. "Yes, sir," said the child, with a voice and manner that showed that her conviction of the truth was perfect.

10. The lawyers asked her many perplexing questions, but she did not vary in the least from her first statement. The truth, as spoken by a little child, was sublime. Falsehood and perjury had preceded her testimony, but before her testimony, falsehood was scattered like chaff.

11. The little child, for whom a mother had prayed for strength to be given her to speak the truth as it was before God, broke the cunning device of matured villainy to pieces, like a potter's vessel.

Moral for Today:

Despite their best efforts, not even a team of lawyers is devious enough to outwit an innocent child schooled in the Ten Commandments.

V. The Way to Be Happy

1. No person can be happy without friends. The heart is formed for love and cannot be happy without it.

2. I have sometimes heard a girl say, "I know that I am very unpopular at school." Now, this plainly shows that she is not amiable.

3. You must not regard it as your misfortune that others do not love you, but your fault. It is not beauty, it is not wealth, that will give you friends. Your heart must glow with kindness if you would attract to yourself the esteem and affection of those around you.

4. If you will adopt the resolution that you will confer favors whenever you can, you will certainly be surrounded by ardent friends.

5. You go to school on a cold winter morning. A bright fire is blazing in the stove, surrounded by boys struggling to get near it to warm themselves. After you are slightly warmed, a schoolmate comes in suffering with cold. "Here, James," you pleas-

antly call out to him, "I am almost warm; you may have my place."

6. As you slip aside to allow him to take your place at the fire, will he not feel that you are kind? The worst boy in the world cannot help admiring such generosity.

7. Suppose, someday, you are out with your companions playing ball. After you have been playing for some time, another boy comes along. He cannot be chosen upon either side, for there is no one to match him. "Henry," you say, "you may take my place a little while, and I will rest."

8. You throw yourself down upon the grass, while Henry, fresh and vigorous, takes your bat and engages in the game. He knows that you gave up to oblige him, and how can he help liking you for it?

9. Look and see which of your companions have the most friends, and you will find that they are those who have this noble spirit, who are willing to deny themselves, that they may make others happy.

Moral for Today:

If you are not particularly attractive, you may need to give away all that you own to make friends. Also your place in a bank line, as you're about to step up to the window. And your tickets to the Super Bowl.

This self-denial for others' enrichment and convenience will enable you to feel true happiness. Just ask the person who gets your new Porsche if you shouldn't be happy about giving it away.

*Y*OU *W*ERE *T*HERE: *C*HARACTER *B*UILDING BY *H*ARDSHIP-*S*IMULATION *E*XERCISES

Don't you feel better already? And we've only been through the formative years!

Now let us reshape your teenage and young adult life through the lifelike application of Hardship Simulations. Terrible adversity! Unbearable cruelty! Anguish and despair! All of which you will learn to rise above. Do they work? Do you think that 747 pilots receive their first lessons trying to land at O'Hare? Of course not. They use simulators so when they crash the plane, it doesn't matter.

Look. Listen. Live each arduous moment.

You're only young once.

Exercise One:
Sharecropper's Apprentice

You are twelve.

Your family lives in the outer reaches of San Antonio, in a structure built of UPS packing boxes joined by brown tape.

Your father, a useless drunkard who knocks out your teeth in mindless rages, has news for you. Today he has sold you to a new family parked in front of your "house" in an old Ford caked with dustbowl grime.

There appear to be at least nine of them in the car. The backseat has been yanked out and replaced by half a worn mattress, where the children play and fight without discipline.

You drive for what seems like days to arrive at a house so humble it actually reminds you of home.

Jake, your new father, pulls you out of the car.

"Don't even think about running away. There's no place to run." You look all around you, and he is obviously right. Absolutely nothing appears as far as you can see but red dirt.

"Now you will learn my trade."

Although the land here seems as infertile as a sheet of tin, your new family earns its living as sharecroppers. Jake's wife, his seven children, and now you too will all pick the crops. Jake himself will supervise.

The first morning you join the rest of your new family hunched over the ground tugging at the crop. You cannot even determine exactly what it is, possibly a turnip of some kind, but it is too covered with dirt to tell. Your back aches horribly from stooping.

Suddenly a tiny tornado of dust blows into your eyes. You try to rub it out with the knuckles of your filthy hands.

Whack! A shattering pain shoots from your tailbone all the way up your spine. You look up into the punishing sun. Your new father and mentor sits tall above a mule which he has fitted with a Western saddle. In his arm he holds a length of two-by-four pine board cradled like a lance.

"Pull!" he commands the mule and it spins around faster than you can blink. Jake has taken accurate aim with the board once again, this time to wallop you precisely in the midsection. You fall screaming to the dirt.

Later you discover that he learned this trick from an overseer at Sugarlands prison farm, while serving a year for stealing TV dinners from a convenience store. Now it is his only real hobby.

"We're going to get along fine," Jake explains fondly. "You'll be the son I never had. And someday, if you do well, all this will be yours."

READY? CHOOSE YOUR RESPONSE.

A. Lose your zest for life and waste away with the blowing dust.

B. Run away to the nearest city.

C. Tough it out and finish school by correspondence course.

THE RIGHT THING TO DO:

A is incorrect. Nobody likes a quitter.

B is incorrect. The only young person more exploited than a sharecropper's apprentice is a teenage runaway.

C is correct. This is what Ross Perot would have done in your place. Adversity builds character and, when the going gets tough, the tough get going.

Exercise Two:
Waiting Tables Where the Cool Kids Eat

You are sixteen and hopelessly in love with a classmate at school.
    You revel in fantasies of the two of you together.
    The air is rich with the possibilities of spring. You sit together on a riverbank under weeping willow trees. The sun is framing your True Love's face with the soft glow of a halo.
    "Hey, we've been here five minutes, y'know? Like, how about some service."

You focus on the whiny voice and see a table of the hateful "Cool Kids" from school. Spoiled, flashing $100 haircuts and $3,500 Cartier Panther watches, unbelievably desirable and sadistic as only teenagers can be. They have come to the seedy restaurant where you work. You can only hope they don't recognize you from school.

"Hey, it's What'saname from homeroom. Real neat apron. So what's good today?"

You want to say, "Grow a brain," or similar. But you bite down hard on your lip and take the guff because this is your *job*. Hateful, humiliating, but your job nevertheless. You only want to scrape a few dollars together to buy a rusted-out Corvair that you can paint, and maybe the cigarette burns on the seats won't be noticeable.

The Cool Kids speak.

"Hey, pay attention, okay? Bring me a medium cheeseburger with everything on it."

"Gimme a shrimp salad. No. Maybe a cheeseburger too. No. Wait a minute. I'm thinking."

You smell something peculiar and notice that, under the table, they're passing around the last of a marijuana joint. If your boss knew, he would fire you for permitting it to happen.

"No smoking at this table. Go outside if you want to do that."

The table is immediately silent. Thick with tension as each of the Cool Kids stares intensely at you. If their eyes were lasers, you would have eight little holes in your forehead.

Suddenly you cannot believe what you see. It is your True Love in the doorway, hair flecked with gold in the sunlight. Eyes as blazing blue as the Caribbean, sparkling with a thousand tiny stars.

Your True Love approaches the table with the Cool Kids, stares at your face for long seconds silently, and finally speaks. "Is that a big zit on your chin, or herpes?"

You feel as if your face were on fire. You walk slowly back to the kitchen, hearing the laughter from the table, and you watch them obviously making fun of you through the little window in the kitchen door.

You hope that, someday, you will be able to show them. You will be rich and famous, they will be burnt-out, filthy heroin addicts you wouldn't touch with an oily rag and a match.

But you know, in your heart, that they will sail through life untouched by pain. Loved but not loving, beautiful and invincible.

And you will probably always be waiting tables wherever they decide to eat.

READY? CHOOSE YOUR RESPONSE.

A. Try to imitate the Cool Kids and be accepted.

B. Save a Cool Kid from drowning and win their respect.

C. Assert your moral superiority over the Cool Kids by challenging them to a bracing round of the Bible Game.

THE RIGHT THING TO DO:

A is incorrect. Your Timex will give you away.

B is incorrect. Stop fantasizing or we will never finish our business here.

C is correct. For instructions on how to play and win the Bible Game, see Chapter Six.

Exercise Three:
A Brutal Hamstring

Because you're a pitiably weak teenager with more guts than muscle or coordination, your high school football coach has placed you with all the other losers on the "bomb squad" during this Friday practice for a Big Game.

This means your task will be to stop the offensive team as it runs down the field toward you with the ball on the first return. Your nemesis, the handsome and brick-solid team captain Doug Dashing, is kicking off, so you'll have to tackle him before he completes his kick.

You long to bring him down into the mud in front of all the kids who have assembled on the sidelines. Just minutes before in the locker room, Dashing jammed you inside your own locker to the delight of the rest of the team, warning you to keep your sorry ass off the field. It seemed as though you were screaming and banging for hours before the coach found you and let you out, barely containing his own amusement.

Now running down the field, panting ferociously, you see Dashing ahead, his face breaking into a smug grin as he notes that you are the one coming for him. But you dart around the opposition one by one, gaining ground. You are now tempered steel, and your only purpose in life is to bring down this blond Viking god who has made your existence on the team a humiliating Hell. You pound ahead, corkscrewing around huge linebackers as if they were tree stumps.

Heart slamming against your ribs in explosive fury, you are now directly on top of Dashing. He is still smiling. You're wondering why, as you take the lunge of your young life—a perfect tackle that connects with the tremendously gratifying sound of Dashing's breath expelled in pain and surprise.

But you also see, in a small corner of your consciousness, the hand he had raised in the air. *Noooo!* your brain screams. He raised his hand in the "fair catch" signal, and you missed it.

What a fool you've made of yourself! What could be worse than this?

Then you feel it. The hamstring muscle in the back of your upper thigh pops like a cork from a bottle, and the massive tugging sensation, the horrible pain of an intense cramp that will not go away, begins. You've pulled your hamstring! The most feared injury of all! Three weeks of excruciating agony, with no end in sight.

READY? CHOOSE YOUR RESPONSE:

A. Scream while you wait for the stretcher.

B. Keep trying to stand, even though you collapse on the dirt every time.

C. Raise your hand toward Dashing and ask for his help in getting up.

THE RIGHT THING TO DO:

A is incorrect. Nobody likes a screamer in contact sports, unless you are a fan.

B is incorrect. Pulling yourself up by your own bootstraps is good, but staying up is better.

C is correct. When he kicks you in response, you will win the grudging sympathy of the spectators after all.

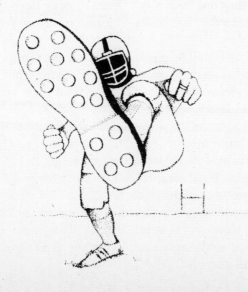

Exercise Four:
Secretary to an Ogre

Your first job out of school involves working for a Senior Vice President of a great multinational corporation.

You show up at nine sharp, Monday morning, and catch the sidelong glances and hushed remarks among the staff. "She's working for Him."

As you near your desk, the office reeks increasingly of tension and thinly veiled loathing. Your desk is pointed out to you by the office manager. She leaves you with the promise, "You will never be bored."

Your desk looks like a recluse's cellar, piled high with memos, telephone messages, unopened mail. The desktop plant is dead. You sit, bewildered. The intercom buzzer rings.

"Come in, hon. Bring the pad."

The boss's office is as large as a ballroom. And foul smelling. A wet cigar rests in the ashtray. Your boss, Mr. Maxwell, sits on an elevated chair behind a large empty desk.

"No, no, no. Not a steno pad. I need my *heating* pad. My back is killing me," he mumbles, letting crumbs from his breakfast roll spill out of his mouth over the napkin tucked into his shirt collar.

"And take that out with you." With a pudgy hand, flashing a diamond pinkie ring, he waves at a pile of laundry piled on a chair.

You hear a high-pitched giggle to your left and see his assistant, a bony and evil-looking young man called Finnerman. Both of them stare at you with no attempt to conceal their inspection of your breasts and legs.

"Are you temporary or permanent?" the fat man at the desk asks through large lips.

"P-p-permanent. I just started this morning."

"Yeah? Maybe. We'll see." He laughs out loud, and Finnerman sneers, a connoisseur of discomfort.

Maxwell pushes back from his desktop and raises his layers of obscene fat to stand. He is short. Practically a dwarf.

"I want these back tomorrow. We're gonna catch a plane for Cleveland. You and me."

You pick up the pile of laundry, and a yellowed undershirt falls on the floor.

"Let me tell you how I work." Maxwell sneers. "We start at seven A.M. I like to get going early, and I take my coffee black. You don't take lunch. I need my phone covered all day long. I expect you to walk around and listen to what people in the office are saying and report to me every day on what you hear. Don't expect to make any friends around here. That's not your job. Your job is to make me look good to the old man.

"I want a daily written report on my desk at seven P.M. Then you can go home. I leave at noon every day. But my boy Finnerman here will call you every night at six fifty-five to make sure you're still here. And you leave a cigar burning in the ashtray so the old man thinks I'm still here too.

"My last gal was a bimbo. I hope you're not, 'cause you'll be writing all my letters. Somebody calls, you tell them I'm in conference. Except the old man. If he calls, you come find me wherever I am, even if I'm in the john. Clear?"

You say something and rush out to your desk, your stomach racked with cold fear.

"Don't forget, honey, Cleveland tomorrow," the hateful little toad shouts after you.

What have I done?

His airline tickets have just arrived, which you open with trembling hands.

The good news: he is booked in first class, and you will ride coach.

"Don't worry." Startled, you turn around to see Maxwell looming over you. "With my frequent flier miles, I'll get you upgraded to sit with me."

His hand rests meaningfully on your shoulder.

READY? CHOOSE YOUR RESPONSE:

A. Sue your boss for sexual harassment under Title VII.

B. Do whatever he says, but complain about him on the Donahue show.

C. Make your relationship an epic struggle between Good and Evil, and make sure you win.

THE RIGHT THING TO DO:

A is incorrect. Nobody likes a litigious person.

B is incorrect. Nobody likes a whiner, either.

C is the only solution, as it also happens to stand for Crusade. Oh, what mighty virtue you can marshal in the cause of Good Business Conduct! Begin tomorrow morning by sneaking a bottle of bourbon and a bottle of L-Triptophane into the office. Put three L-Triptophane capsules into his morning coffee. When he dozes off at his desk, pour plenty of bourbon down his shirtfront and drop him onto the floor. Put the half-empty bottle in his bottom desk drawer. Close his door and have a discreet discussion with the office manager. He will be shipped off that very day to a Care Unit for at least thirty days, during which time your services will be requested by all the nice executives on the floor for your superb discretion. What a triumph for the forces of Good! Bravo!

Exercise Five:
Marine Boot Camp

It is now the sixth day since you were brought to Parris Island by bus, packed in with a load of small-town bullies, trembling boys with acne, plump apple-cheeked farm kids, scarecrow-like junior drifters from dirt patches in Oklahoma, and urban sociopaths with giant radios on their shoulders blasting at 50,000 decibels.

You clearly remember with satisfaction how those radios were smashed to the pavement and stomped on by the screaming Drill Instructors as they pulled you and the others off the bus by your hair, limbs, necks, whatever was handy.

You vividly recall the way the Senior Drill Instructor made you stand on the little yellow feet painted onto the asphalt. And how he leaned into you until his contorted red leather face with the crudely stitched stab wound across his forehead and the angry popping veins couldn't have been more than one-sixteenth of an inch away from your face, as he screamed questions at you laced with spittle. Questions you could not seem to answer correctly no matter what you replied.

But gradually you made sense of this strange redneck's Socratic method, as you grew used to other aspects of Marine life. You learned to read The Little Red Book of Marine philosophy standing at attention, going to parade rest position wherever you turned a page, then snapping back to attention again. You figured out how to effectively clean the platoon's row of urinals with a toothbrush when ordered, which was often.

You even braced yourself to suffer the Parris Island sand fleas in your eyes or nostrils when you stood at attention. Because, when you flinched and swatted one, your D.I. explained that having killed the sand flea, you would have to give it a proper burial. First you had to find the flea's remains. Then you dug a six-foot grave, placed the flea corpse inside, and covered it with a dirt mound. Next your D.I. decided he didn't like the burial location. So you had to dig up the flea's grave, find the flea corpse again in the dirt, and bury it two yards farther down the hill.

Tonight as you doze off on your hard metal bunk, disturbed only by the snoring of an adenoidal youngster from New Jersey, you think that just maybe you will survive this indescribably hellish ordeal. One day soon you will even look like a real Marine. A real Marine! In dress blues and polished brass . . .

"Flood! Flood!" The screams came from all around you. You sit bolt upright with your eyes blazing open in the darkness. You can't make out a thing.

"There's a flood here, you miserable maggots!"

You recognize the voice of your Senior D.I.

"Get your lockers and your putrid selves up on the top bunks before you drown."

You find your locker in the dark and try to heft it up to the top locker, but the damnable heavy chest falls all the way down onto your left foot, breaking at least one of your toes. Your screams are hardly noticed in the black din, as shoving, terrorized bodies clamor for the high ground.

Finally you drag your locker and your wounded toe up to the top bunk, where a dimwitted kid thrashes about, squealing like a scalded ferret. But at least you made it up before the flood swept you and your locker away.

"Hurricane! Climb down to low ground, you stupid maggots!"

Hurricane? You think you must not have heard your D.I. properly, and freeze rabbit-style in the glare of a flashlight.

"Well, you little maggot," your Senior D.I. snarls. "Guess you're going to get your whole platoon killed because you can't move fast enough. There's some reason you don't have sense enough to crawl down to low ground when a hurricane's coming, PRIVATE MAGGOT??"

This requires your prompt reply.

READY: CHOOSE YOUR RESPONSE

A. "First you said there's a flood and now you say there's a hurricane. I'm all confused."

B. "Sir! No, Sir!"

C. "Sir, the Private takes offense and respectfully challenges the Drill Instructor to a duel with pistols to the death, if the Captain gives his permission, Sir!"

THE RIGHT THING TO DO:

A is incorrect, maggot.

B is incorrect. Failing to impress the Senior D.I. at this critical point will subject you to as loathsome a punishment as he has had years to dream up.

C is correct. If the Captain gives his permission, practice your marksmanship.

▪ ▪ ▪ ▪ ▪ ▪

*B*ONUS! *B*ONUS! *B*ONUS!
*E*XTRA *C*OMMAND *P*OINTS!

For answering Exercise Five correctly, you have just earned promotion to Bonus Exercise Six . . .

Officer's Candidate School (OCS): The Square M.B.A.!

Here's a military leadership scenario for you to perform all by yourself. Good luck, and godspeed. (Just don't screw up, maggot, 'cause you have American lives in your hands.)

Official OCS War Game: Invasion of "Club Red," Martinique

SITUATION:

U.S. Army Intelligence reports confirm the existence of Cuban military advisers on the island of Martinique, running a phony resort cleverly camouflaged to resemble Club Med.

Unsuspecting American tourists who believe they are being picked up at the Martinique airport by Club Med personnel are transported by Cuban soldiers in body sarongs and beads to "Club Red."

There trained communists of both sexes seduce the Americans, fill their heads with propaganda, and send them home as espionage agents.

OPTIONS

Scenario 1: Enter an official U.S. protest through the United Nations General Assembly, which is controlled by anti-American zealots.

Scenario 2: Use military assets to destroy Club Red, Martinique, and save its American captives.

CODE NAME: OPERATION BEACHFRONT
12 March, 0600 hrs.
President approves Scenario 2 and orders Beachfront invasion plan, orchestrated by Joint Chiefs of Staff.

12 March, 0610 hrs.

As officer-in-command of the air strike force, you are busy with:

1. Reconnaissance via AWAC to gather intelligence on enemy positions and activities.
2. Cutting off supply routes to "Club Red" from local hotel kitchens.
3. Attacking enemy ground forces with missile-launching Air Cavalry helicopters.
4. Airfield strikes on Martinique airport to remove landing facilities for enemy support troops.
5. Maintaining air superiority via squadron of Navy F-14 Tomcats.

12 March, 1100 hrs.

You are besieged with problems.

Your AWACs aircraft has identified fourteen American women held prisoner by Cuban soldiers in a thatched roof shack within the "Club Red" perimeter. Instead of their trying to escape, electronic surveillance picks up their threats to defend the village against your strike force because "American men are jerks."

Your airfield strikes have taken out a runway about to be used by an Air France 747 full of Parisians on holiday. Its captain arrogantly insists on circling over Martinique until you let him land, despite warnings from your F-14 Tomcats.

The Cuban officer in command, who speaks fluent English, is holding a press conference, televised worldwide. He claims that he and his troops were only on vacation there when you attacked, and he questions your personal manhood.

Now what do you do?

■■■■■■

READY? CHOOSE YOUR RESPONSE:

A. Call for a tactical nuke strike.

B. Send in the Navy Seals for hand-to-hand combat on the beach.

C. Go in yourself, unarmed, and challenge the Cuban leader to single combat—just you and him—at 0600 hours (6:00 A.M.) sharp tomorrow.

THE RIGHT THING TO DO:

A is incorrect. We don't have our officer's thinking cap on today, do we?

B is incorrect. Nobody likes an armchair general.

C is correct. No Caribbean-born officer will show up on time for combat promptly at 6:00 A.M. Now you may declare victory by default at 0601, with plenty of television news coverage for all the world to see.

Congratulations. You made it through the first hurdle of early physical and emotional hardship.

Feeling stronger? Now let's grow wittier and wiser.

three

*T*HIRTY *M*INUTES TO *A*DULT *W*IT & *W*ISDOM

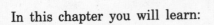

■ ■ ■ ■ ■ ■

In this chapter you will learn:

■ the never-revealed secret of grown-up humor.

■ the Presidential-wit mystery and coverup.

■ the adult truths that will set you free from your insecurities.

■ how to reason with the trained accuracy of an adult WASP.

■ how to be listened to whenever you decide to speak.

*P*art of growing up, a necessary condition of getting un-hip, involves changing your mind about (1) what you think is funny and (2) what you think you know.

Barefaced adult hypocrisy no longer seems funny (indeed, appears quite functional), but reading in *The Wall Street Journal* that a high school classmate lost the million dollars he made at age twenty-one by marketing a novelty "pet ulcer" may produce a hearty chuckle.

One also recognizes that the smug, know-it-all satisfaction of youth stems from almost total ignorance, particularly of How Things Really Work in the adult world. Now, some may worry that gaining adult awareness of How Things Really Work will produce lingering stabs of wounded vanity, unbridled rage at life's unfairness, and a bitter, weeping melancholia. This represents a textbook fear, not unfounded, of the adult unknown.

Recognizing your likely distaste for taking important new information cold in the face, let us begin on a note of levity.

*A*DULT *H*UMOR: *I*T *I*SN'T *F*UNNY

One might presume that adult wit ages and improves over the years, with a finer appreciation of humor enjoyed less frequently.

In fact, the opposite holds true.

Responsible adulthood brings with it such a yoke of unrelenting concern for others that adults emit a continuing silent scream for the release of humor. Anything that lets adults blow off a well-earned chortle or belly laugh will be a festive occasion all by itself.

Observe the Humor Maturation Chart on pages 75–78.

Since young children become wildly amused by what goes wrong in an otherwise orderly existence, such as a Thanksgiving turkey brought out of the oven that, slipping through Mother's fingers, crashes to the floor, splattering everyone with hot pieces of stuffing and cranberries, they read comic books, or "funny books" that depict such phenomena.

During puberty, children develop rebellious tendencies satisfied through the mild satire of *Mad* magazine. *Mad* supports its now white-bearded founders by continuing to parody Republicanism and Madison Avenue, just as it did in the early 1950s, so is recommended as the only middle-aged humor source for teenagers.

■ ■ ■ ■ ■ ■

HUMOR MATURATION CHART

■ ■ ■ ■ ■ ■

Stage:

Teenage-volume
rebellion

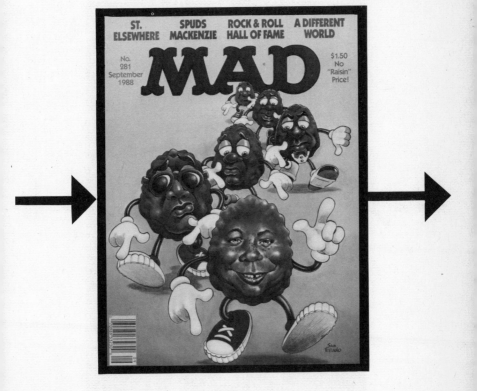

Stage:

Punkish irreverence
and scatological rutting

Stage:

Establishment entry-level
mores and values

"Tell me, sir, is there any such thing as just a plain
Republican, or are they all staunch?"

Stage:

Fully matured
adult humor

The nose-thumbing and sniggering prurience of teenagers reach their climax during the college years, when *National Lampoon* becomes oh-so-appealing for its "hip" mix of scatological humor, exposed breasts, new wave cartooning, and sneering irreverence toward every institution that responsible adults cherish.

Once socialized by exposure to the world of work, marriage, and family, the young adult is soothed by Eastern Establishment cartoons.

Ultimately the square adult will settle comfortably into the *Reader's Digest,* with low-impact humor of particular interest to the Restoration Era, such as "Life in These United States" and "Humor in Uniform," and the safe yucks of old Andy Hardy movies.

However, knowing *how* adult behavior develops does not address the critical question of *what* is funny.

THE ROOT OF MOST ADULT HUMOR

Perhaps you recall a time when you were invited into the Principal's office, no doubt to receive some Good Conduct badge, at the same time that a bad boy or girl had been called in for severe punishment.

"Oh, yes." The Principal beams upon seeing you. "Now just a minute and we'll be right with you."

Suddenly his smiling countenance changed to one of scowling rage as he turned to the other child. "You, Albert, march in here RIGHT NOW!"

And little Albert, intestinal juices loudly bubbling away, shuffled into God-only-knows-what fate behind the slammed door.

Didn't you feel a delicious tingle of excitement and, yes, irrepressible nervous *giggling* which you found almost impossible to control? Authority missed you this time and singled out another child for terrible retribution.

What a hoot!

This source of childhood fun lingers well into adulthood and forms the conceptual basis for what adults think of as funny, which is embarrassment or fear at someone else's plight turned into nervous laughter.

Since it would be unseemly for mature adults to admit to such an uncharitable expression of glee, the comedic principle has come to be known by other names.

There is the *comedy of manners,* which attempts to laugh away the embarrassing clash of people with different mores or social class origins, or *self-effacing humor,* which addresses the embarrassing incompetence of people who hold positions of responsibility and authority, or *adult prurience,* which is embarrassment over repressed sexual matters considered taboo for polite conversation.

The Comedy of Manners
(Slobs vs. Snobs)

The "Comedy of Manners" tradition extends from eighteenth-century England, in plays such as *She Stoops to Conquer, or, The Mistakes of a Night* by Oliver Goldsmith (1728–1774), explaining the possibilities for embarrassment when a young aristocrat mistakes his prospective father-in-law for a common innkeeper and his prospective fiancée for a tavern wench. This tradition has enriched contemporary American comedy, reaching its apotheosis in *Animal House* by Beard and Kenny (1976), cataloging the opportunities for embarrassment when a fraternity of common "slobs" pits itself against the establishment "snobs" (Dean, fraternity, ROTC leadership, and local town government), creating much mirth.

Curiously, one may enjoy a good titter from the Comedy of Manners as both a teenager and an adult. Except as an adult, you will gradually find yourself rooting for the "snobs," and wishing that their "slob" persecutors could be held in detention camps until they grow up.

For illustration, here is a short comedy of manners from the more satisfying adult point of view.

Example: "Establishment House"

At Haverford College the Dean and his wife, Elise, are entertaining Diane, the Sorority Council President, and Bill, a student officer of the ROTC chapter, as well as other students of good character at the Dean's campus home, Establishment House.

ELISE
(winking):   Bill, I believe you have some exciting news to share with us.

BILL: Yes, ma'am. I've asked Diane to marry me before I join NATO in Europe, and I'm proud to say that she's accepted!

Diane flashes a tasteful diamond-and-emerald engagement ring, to the oohs and aahs of all assembled.

> DEAN: That's wonderful news, Bill and Diane. And we have a surprise for you, too!

The lights dim, and a servant wheels out a handsome cake lit with sparklers. Again, admiring oohs and aahs celebrate the moment.

Suddenly the French doors break open, and a fat, sloppily dressed youth with matted hair and protruding eyeballs crashes into the room. It is Blotto, a member of the ill-esteemed "animal house" fraternity on campus.

Blotto grabs a handful of the beautiful cake and jams it into his mouth, then pops his full cheeks with his palms so that the frothy cake flies out onto the tabletop and guests.

> BLOTTO: Aaargh! Food Fight, everybody!

The assembled guests dab off the bits of cake from their suits with napkins and continue to converse as if Blotto were not in the room.

> ELISE: So, Bill, what's the nature of your assignment with NATO?

> BLOTTO
> *(before Bill
> can reply)*: He's gonna be an Intelligence Officer! We found his orders in the dumpster outside the ROTC building! A guy who's too dumb to find the soap in a shower!

> DEAN
> *(turning to
> Blotto)*: You may not realize it, son, but your admission of snooping into classified government documents has just entitled you to arrest under provisions of the Official Secrets Act!

> BILL: Gentlemen, take your prisoner.

The kitchen door opens to reveal two burly MPs, who pick the astonished Blotto up off his feet and hustle him out the French doors, reading him his rights as a federal prisoner as they go.

BLOTTO *(screaming back)*:	I saw your fiancée naked! I saw her in her room in the sorority house with her jugs out!
DIANE:	I really must get curtains for that window.
DEAN:	You needn't worry about that anymore, Diane. We have the proof we need to close down that boy's fraternity now. They think they're having a toga party tonight, but they'll be receiving some unexpected guests from the FBI.
BILL:	I guess the French would call *that* party a *fête accompli!*

Hearty laughter fills the room, and toasts to Diane and Bill are offered all around.

SELF-EFFACING HUMOR

The reason that few non-adults master this form is simply that they have few accomplishments to be humble and self-effacing about. Thus all their humor directs itself at others' frailties in order to pump up their own fragile egos.

Self-effacing humor remains the playground of the enlarged and healthy egos of the rich, powerful, and authoritative. Henry Kissinger or William F. Buckley comes to mind. Look at all they've done in life! All the triumphs! All the accolades they've received! And they can still mumble a self-deprecatory comment that pricks the huge dirigible of achievement that hangs proudly overhead wherever they speak.

How sporting of them to share a good one with us (we who thought they were just pompous bigwigs). Ha! Good show!

Example:

The Duty of Citizens with Regard to Presidential Humor

Presidential humor is, of course, the zenith of "self-effacing wit."

In no office does it become as essential to the national interest to be laughed *with* instead of *at* as when one occupies the Oval Office.

Rule #1: Presidents aren't supposed to be very funny people, and they generally meet this expectation.

Rule #2: Presidents possess the same basic incompetencies as other adults and thus employ humor to distract us from what would otherwise be a horrifying, full-fledged realization of their bungling or dimwitted malpractice.

Rule #3: It's better for both of us, President and citizen, to pretend they're funny. This explains the great roar of hilarity even among the White House press corps when a President attempts the most modest stab at humor.

Here are some examples of actual Presidential wit from the good (Republican) Presidents.

President Reagan on Trying to Remember One Darn Thing or Another:

Reporter: You said that you would resign if your memory started to go.

Reagan: When did I say that?

President Ford, on Answering President Johnson's Charge That He Cannot Walk and Chew Gum at the Same Time:
"The White House was preparing for Ford's appearance at a correspondents' dinner at which the guest of honor would be comedian Chevy Chase. For two years Chase had been ridiculing, on *Saturday Night Live,* Jerry Ford's clumsiness, showing him walking into doors and falling down stairs. . . . At the Chevy Chase dinner the stage was set. The President was introduced. 'I was standing there and I saw it happen,' said [joke writer Dan] Penny. 'The President got up from the table and dropped about sixty pounds of silver all over the floor. . . . People were screaming. . . . And he played it beautifully! He said, "Oh, my gosh . . . oh, shucks . . . oh, sorry . . ." And nobody realized it was set up. . . . Then he got up there and did the whole speech bit, which worked magnificently! And then he just smiled, and he said, "Good evening, I'm Gerald Ford," and he turned to Chevy Chase and said, "And you're not." ' "

> From Gerald Gardner, *All the Presidents' Wits* (New York: William Morrow, 1986), p. 129.

President Nixon Observed Trying to Make a Note to Himself and Speak to His Aides at the Same Time:
"His desk was neat and spotless . . . but his thoughts and actions were far from organized. Whenever he wanted to make a note to himself, he would go through a long and awkward ritual. First he would put on his dark-rimmed glasses. Then he would reach into a vest pocket to fish for an envelope or a scrap of paper. Simultaneously he would reach into the opposite vest pocket with his other hand to find his pen. The required objects would often elude his grasp, leaving the President struggling, his arms crossed in front of himself. Finally he would pull out the fountain pen, bite off the top, and hold it in his teeth as he scrawled with some difficulty on the scrap of paper he clutched in the palm of one hand. . . . Such episodes, plus the obtuse conversations, gradually humanized Richard Nixon for me."

> From John Dean, *Blind Ambition* (New York: Simon & Schuster, 1976), p. 184.

ADULT PRURIENCE: A NEW BEGINNING

In the Restoration Era humor will take a more prurient turn through the self-denial of normal sexual activity, which must be sublimated into New-Puritan obsessions, such as making sure several times a day that one's desk is in PERFECT ORDER and joking about acts which one is too inhibited to come right out and request.

Since the watershed film *Fatal Attraction* exposed extramarital sex as an opportunity to wind up with something terrible that one cannot seem to get rid of, interest in the opposite sex has plummeted on a straight-line down-trend, while interest in the same sex has held its similarly downward course since the AIDS epidemic achieved national publicity.

This long-term trending will inspire a reawakened interest in sexual partners carrying no threat of AIDS, PMS, or biological ticking. The objects of lust in the nineties thus promise to be either animal, mineral, or vegetable. And it will be these objects of affection that dominate prurient-interest jokes for adults.

Example: How to Tell a Bestiality Joke in Mixed Company

A young fellow was sailing his 41-foot Morgan far out in the Bahamas when he hit a reef and was forced to swim to shore.

There he found a deserted island with nothing on it but a sheep and a mangy cur of a sheepdog.

Well, eventually the fellow became . . . er . . . interested in the sheep and began making (ahem) advances toward it. But each time he came close, the dog would raise a terrible fuss, growling and snapping at the young man and refusing to let him come near.

Well, this went on for weeks and weeks. Until one morning the young fellow was gazing out toward the sea and, lo and behold, he saw another boat caught up on the same darned reef, and a small rubber dinghy making its way to his island.

Who should come ashore but a beautiful young woman of . . . ah . . . the full-figured variety.

She looked around and asked, "Are we the only ones here?"
The young man nodded. She said, "Well, in that case, is there
anything I can . . . uh . . . *do* . . . for you?"

"There sure is," the young man replied. "Can you take this dog
for a walk?"

"I Wish I'd Said That"

If you have ever uttered that lament, you can clearly see the
problem of *cleverness* as a source of adult humor.

Since few can master it, the ability to do so breeds a deep-
seated envy and distrust in the many who cannot.

Cleverness, in a nation where half the population has earned
an IQ score under 100, is in many quarters considered undemo-
cratic and its corollary, un-American.

Hence the familiar expression, "Too clever for his/her own good,"
with the dark hint of a lynch mob lurking to rush the clever one
outside at the next artful turn of phrase.

Clever, snappy repartee may be best confined to the ranks of
the literati/glitterati as they meet for dinner in restaurants fre-
quented by foreigners, out preening one another in both trendy
dress and hip *bon mots*.

Cleverness is not square; thus will be frowned upon, if not made
an actual civil offense, in the Restoration Era.

Example: The Cavett Curse

While many hip persons professed to enjoy the slyness and wit of
Dick Cavett, he failed to earn the love of the larger and infinitely
more powerful Square Establishment.

Thus, his talk show was shunted from commercial television
to public television, until he disappeared altogether from the home
screen, only to turn up on Broadway acting in the occasional
Harold Pinter play.

Why? Terminal cleverness afflicted this otherwise promising lad, who hailed from the same Nebraska soil as Johnny Carson.

Cavett possessed qualities of nervousness sufficient to embarrass legions of viewers, which was good. But he also contracted the need to have the last word, which was bad.

> *A woman wearing a black leather jacket accosts me.*
> *She is not dainty. A small section of her blue jeans has*
> *been sandpapered away to reveal a tattoo on her upper*
> *thigh—something like a snake being struck by light-*
> *ning. You might cast her as female bouncer in a bowl-*
> *ing alley. She is trouble.*
> *"Well, well, if it isn't Dickie Cavett."*
> *"Then who is it?" I reply ill-advisedly. Something*
> *about this kind of opening makes me want to light out*
> *for the territory immediately, and also makes me*
> *want to stay and match so-called wits to amuse the*
> *onlookers. . . .*

"Some friends of mine," she goes on, *"came over to get your autograph in Howard Johnson's yesterday and you were snotty to them . . . all I want to hear from you is an apology."*

"I'm afraid you're going to need extremely acute hearing."

(Whereupon she no doubt identified herself as a network executive, who bounced Cavett into public broadcasting.)

From Dick Cavett and Christopher Porterfield, *Eye on Cavett* (New York: Arbor House, 1983), p. 58.

ADULT WISDOM: THE TRUTHS ONLY WE KNOW FOR SURE

Let's take a deep breath.

That's good. Now back in your seat, please, to receive the momentarily painful, but ultimately comfortable, mantle of adult wisdom.

First it may be helpful to perform a personal inventory of your current knowledge and experience by taking out a clean sheet of paper and printing, legibly, your answers to the six Big Adult Questions:

1. What is the meaning of my life?

2. Who really controls things?

3. Who is the smartest person in the world?

4. Will I ever meet my perfect "soulmate"?

5. Why is life unfair?

6. Is the platinum card worth the extra money?

Thank you. Regrettably, your answers betray a woefully inadequate understanding of How Things Really Work.
Read carefully, now, and don't try to skim.

What Is the Meaning of My Life?

Whether or not you believe in an ultimate heavenly reward for doing what is right, rest assured that you will writhe in eternal hellfire for doing otherwise.

Your every move is observed through life, your every thought heard, your nasty little secrets are well known and duly recorded in a personal file so voluminous as to make you squirm and redden with shame on every page. The times you were mean to other children, lied to your parents, misbehaved as a teenager and didn't get caught, were sloppy in your work and blamed it on someone else, avoided the poor co-worker who got fired when you could have eased a fellow human being's misery, and turned the page on charitable appeals from needy children who do not share your good fortune.

But don't let that upset you, because you still have time to reverse your current course, maybe, because Heaven knows the first part of your life is a sorry shambles. Right your wrongs, correct your egregious faults, do what's correct instead of what's convenient, and do something about your constant preoccupation with sex.

Meaning? For goodness' sake, get your house in order and then we can talk about "meaning."

Who Really Controls Things

Do you know who was really responsible for making people stand in long gas lines in 1979 to jack up the price of oil and realize windfall profits?

Did you ever wonder who was behind the stock market crash in '87?

Have you questioned why the covers of supposedly competing *Time* and *Newsweek* look exactly the same so often?

You think it was *us?* The Establishment?? You must be joking.

Brace yourself for the brisk chill of reality.

The *Japanese* cleverly bought out every drop of Arab oil and kept it from the American people, pursuing the long-term strategy of flooding the U.S. market with their sneaky little cars.

The *Swiss* fiendishly created the crash of '87 to win back the international investors they had been losing to the U.S. bull market. Proof: Read Paul Erdman's *The Crash of '89,* cleverly mistitled to throw thoughtful readers off the track.

The *Russians* have carefully fashioned an international conspiracy of left-leaning journalists, who consistently hound and humiliate the American establishment, while fondly portraying the Yuppie dictator Gorbachev and his wife, Raisa. Further proof: Does Andy Rooney ever have anything *good* to say about American life?

Who Is the Smartest Person in the World?

Perhaps you have heard dull-normal people begin some argument with "I may not be the smartest person in the world, but it seems to me . . ."

Wouldn't it be instructive to know who the smartest person in the world *is,* so you could finally receive a definitive answer to every burning question on your mind?

The fact is that the smartest person in the world may right now be pushing a plow led by oxen through a rice paddy in Cambodia, never having taken an I.Q. test, because high intelligence is randomly distributed throughout the population.

But the important fact is that it doesn't even matter. Intelligence without character and American can-do is no scholar for achievement.

The highest I.Q. scores recorded by a population were the Japanese born in 1960 and 1961, 10 percent of whom scored over genius level of 130. Yet what have *they* accomplished other than building a lot of Suzuki Samurais and playing Pachinko?

A simple anecdote will illustrate the useless nature of egghead intelligence without moral backbone:

The smartest man in the world was flying in a small plane with a priest and a young student. Suddenly the plane developed engine trouble and went spiraling toward earth.

"Well," said the smartest man in the world, "I count three of us but only two parachutes. Since I am the smartest man in the world, you must understand why I need to save myself for the good of humanity!"

And, squirming into the straps of the first parachute he saw, he jumped out of the plane without a word of farewell.

"Father, what shall we do now?" asked the young student. "We have only one parachute left between us!"

"Don't worry, my son," replied the priest. "The smartest man in the world just jumped out of the plane with your knapsack on."

Will I Ever Meet My Perfect "Soulmate"?

Yes, you are 99 percent certain to meet the person who shares your exact background, values, and interests, who dreams your dreams, is both attractive and sensitive, thoughtful but not moody or difficult, and would care about you more than any other human being in the world.

Unfortunately, because things don't always happen as you would wish, you will be most likely to meet that person in a situation something like this:

YOU: Excuse me, I think I'm next in line.

SOULMATE: Well, if it's that important to you, go ahead. *(Walks off in a huff and out of your life forever.)*

Why Is Life Unfair?

Now we get down to it. Although your attitudes and behavior may be carefully observed and recorded, this does not mean that there will be a perfect measure of goodness repaid to you for every decent thing you do.

Consider Job, who led a righteous life, yet he lost his wife, his home was ravaged by locusts, he was covered with boils, and all the rest. Then he whined incessantly about it under the theory that good people should not be forced to suffer. Well, can you imagine what could have happened to Job if he had *not* been a good person? What if he cheated a gang of Philistines in some business deal, and they tied his four limbs to different chariots and sent them thundering off in all directions? What if he got too close while stoning a leper and had to worry (inaccurately, yet) for the rest of his life about catching the disease?

We all know people who've had problems like Job, and that's why we have no shortage of insurance companies in the United States to cover loss of life and property damage.

No, there isn't a Cosmic Scale of fairness to mete out rewards and punishments, but only the churning universe of random events. Job's wife got sick from one of the many pestilences stalking the land. Job's house happened to be where the locusts were swarming that day. The boils appeared as a normal reaction to stress.

Your soulmate will never get to know you because, in a world of four billion people, the odds are stacked against you.

Someone much less deserving may get rich instead of you, simply because there are seventy million people in the United States between twenty-five and forty, many of whom share your ambition, your greed, your hopes, your unique ideas.

You could easily be the next victim of a demented terrorist attack, just by taking the wrong cruise ship to the Caribbean.

There are only five ways to feel secure in this unpredictable showering of random atrocities, this minefield of uncertainty:

1. Stay close to home. In it if possible.

2. Stick to those you know. Family, preferably.

3. Trust no one but other New Establishment members, and none too implicitly.

4. Don't experiment with exotic foreign foods.

5. If you must travel, carry the American Express platinum card.

Is the Platinum Card Worth the Extra Money?

Yes, as a shield against the horror of unimagined events.

For example, an executive who carried the platinum card took ill in Europe and could not be treated adequately in a local hospital. As a platinum card holder, he was rushed by helicopter ambulance to a proper facility and received expensive treatment there, at a cost of over $100,000, all courtesy of American Express.

However, it is considered bad form when dining with square companions to flash a status-conferring "executive" card. Instead, one should ask the waiter whether dinner can be charged to a Sears card.

LUNATIC FRINGE DEPARTMENT:
Rational Explanations for Square Phenomena

Over the years, self-styled investigators have advanced bizarre theories to explain perfectly natural events, which have been spread by irresponsible media to infect public belief.

Since adult wisdom means recognizing that childish fantasies of "ancient astronauts" and "UFOs" have no place in responsible thought, here are the rational explanations for three of these so-called unexplained phenomena.

Squares from Outer Space?

In 1971 a Tempe, Arizona, retired couple claims to have taken this photograph of an "unidentified flying object." The *National Enquirer* ran the photograph the same year with the misleading headline, "Squares from Outer Space?"

Rational Explanation: It was a U.S. Navy weather balloon.

The Bermuda Square

In 1980 it was reported that a total of 262 cruise ships had sailed into the body of water surrounding Bermuda, but only 260 returned to their home ports.

What happened to the missing ships?

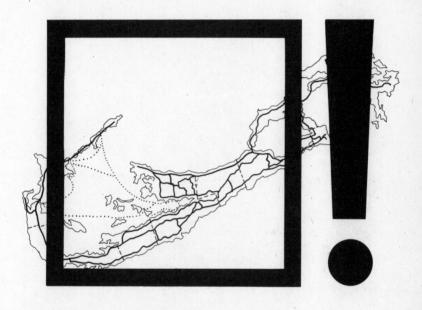

Rational Explanation: They must have vanished.

The Square Heads of Easter Island

In the 1880s anthropologists discovered that the ancient Square Heads of Easter Island were more than forty feet high and weighed twenty tons each.

How did the natives erect the huge stone heads more than two thousand years ago, without benefit of modern engineering?

Rational Explanation: Superman visited Easter Island disguised as Clark Kent.

MAKING PERFECT SENSE

Even the most casual survey of modern discourse will conclude that most adults base their discussions and arguments on irrational, emotional, and childish premises. So their conclusions are invariably founded on four propositions:

1. "I want . . ." (or "don't want")

2. "I like . . ." (or "don't like")

3. "I need . . ." (or "don't need")

4. "I know . . ." (never "I don't know")

This means in practice that the responsible adult will, like Captain Furillo of "Hill Street Blues," continually need to settle conflicting wants or ideas held by narcissistic adults.

Fortunately, the proved mechanism of Irrefutable WASP Logic exists to handle these squabbles, and its principles are easily learned.

WASP Logic:
The Seven Stages of Rational Thought

1. **What's the problem here?** This intervention of self is approached in the parental manner of a concerned Hugh Beaumont sensing a tiff between Wally and the Beaver. This establishes one's authority to sort out the relevant facts from the emotional outbursts sure to follow.

   "Ethel stole my quarterly report for her business plan!"
   "I did not!"
   "You did too!!"

2. *I'll handle this.* Authority established, you position yourself over the combatants as both arbiter and, ultimately, judge, whose wisdom will be accepted and adhered to. A stern demeanor adds credibility, as does a long, hard look in the eyes of each participant, which clearly telegraphs, "Make my day."

3. *Suppressing emotional issues.* The immature enjoy treating every difference of opinion as an opportunity to bring up personal likes and dislikes, who said what to whom, pent-up feelings about irrelevant topics, and all the other emotional paraphernalia they drag with them as they make their noisy way through life.

   Your job as WASP logician involves stripping away each layer of sticky emotion until the bare facts are finally exposed.

   "Ahem . . . well, it says here on Ethel's memo to you dated October 9 that she would require your figures for her plan."

   "See? It's just like Ethel to sneak something like that in a memo she knows I wouldn't read . . . (etc.)"

4. *Showing no favoritism.* Perceptions of favoritism and politics will always fan the immature into a white heat, so it becomes critical to apply your truth-seeking evenhandedly.

   "John, I don't believe you've told your side of the story."

   "Why should I? After all, they promoted Ethel instead of me because she's a girl."

5. *Resisting personal motives.* No matter how mightily you detest either party, or how much you stand to gain from a particular outcome, you must never, *ever,* let your personal motives intrude into the sacred thousand-year heritage of honor-driven WASP logic!

6. *Withholding judgment.* Just when you think you have made up your mind, set your opinion aside. Go duck hunting for a day and let it sit with you awhile. Mix a good stiff bourbon and cogitate on it in your study. Stay awake at night and let the responsibility really get to you.

7. *Managing high blood pressure.* Whatever conclusion you arrive at via logic, many (including you) may find it abhorrent.

IF: Ethel advised John in writing that she would need his report.

THEN: John had a duty to make it available to her.

ERGO: Though Ethel may be a dangerous and disagreeable little mongoose, she clearly has John on a cold reading of the relevant facts.

Do you feel the yoke of responsibility tightening? Growing heavier on your shoulders?

Thank Heaven the second half of making perfect sense is much easier, relying more on your ability to simply keep still.

The Conversational Arts

Doubtless you've noticed that all those around you seem to spend most of their time talking, primarily about themselves. It's as if a conversational marathon were in progress, with an all-expense paid lifetime tour of the spas and pleasure domes of the world awarded to the yammering soul who can outtalk, outquip, outquestion, and outshout the other 239,999,999 people in the United States.

SHAKEN MAN: I have bad news for all of you. My doctor just told me I'm shrinking six inches every day and I'll soon be gone.

HIS BEST FRIEND: Really? That's nothing! I had a friend who . . .

HIS WIFE: You know what that reminds me of? On the "Tonight Show" this guy told a joke . . .

HIS CHILD: That's like this show I saw Saturday morning where the Masters of the Universe . . .

HIS BROTHER-IN-LAW: Oh, yeah? Well, let me tell you something, I read about a woman who . . .

Saying Nothing

In the midst of this cacophony of voices struggling to be heard first, most, and best, it will be the responsible adult's lot to keep silent most of the time, speaking only when one has something to say.

If you think that a person would be trampled to death today by following this course, you will be delighted to learn the final Adult Truth:

People listen more closely to those who speak less, under the same principles of novelty and scarcity that prompt them to buy products that are in shorter supply.

Ha! Imagine yourself at a meeting full of posing, bleating juveniles, verbally shoving to be heard above the rest, when suddenly you, who have sat like the Great Stone Sphinx of Egypt for forty-seven minutes, suddenly lean forward perceptively and raise one finger slightly above your folded hands. Shocked, the combatants turn and wonder, "What is the silent Sphinx, that wonder of the world, going to say?"

A hush falls over the room as you speak softly:

"We have two clear options."

Only two? Out of all the opinions and scenarios voiced at this contentious meeting? They lean closer and strain to hear what you have to say.

Letting Fools Rush In

By remaining hawklike above the verbal fray, you could swoop down at leisure and pick whatever bits of truth dropped from the forty-five minutes of self-hype provided by the other participants. This is known as "letting fools rush in (where wise men fear to tread)."

Now you only need to summarize any two positions, evaluate them coldly, and offer a recommendation.

Advising Caution

One of the greatest joys of responsible adulthood experienced in both business and social or home life is advising caution when someone else makes a foolish, headstrong remark that may lead to imprudent action.

CHEERLEADER: Kill State! Kill State!

YOU
(rising from
bleachers):   Now, hold on a minute . . .

Since immaturity demands immediate gratification for every
whim, you will have no shortage of opportunities to practice this
restraint.

Measured Replies

Closely akin to advising caution is the carefully considered reply
that falls short of total, gung-ho agreement with whatever fool-
ishness or personal opinion you have been asked to join.

FRIEND: It's just not right for Jennie to clean out our
joint bank account, sell our house out from
under me, and take the kids with her to
Denmark, so she could move in with a sev-
enteen-year-old guy she met at a sex
show . . . is it?

YOUR RESPONSE
(delivered after
thirty seconds of
thought):   "Right" is an awfully strong word, Dick.

Better to think about such matters for several days before passing judgment.

Making Soothing Noises

Since you will be withholding your judgment in *all* cases laden
with emotional content, you will need to master the perfect-sense
alternative known as "making soothing noises."

1. Listen to audio tapes of pigeons cooing, the rush of the "ocean" inside a seashell, and especially the teddy bear that approximates sounds from a pregnant mother's womb, to get the proper rhythm.

2. Lower your voice a full octave.

3. Practice saying the following:

   "There, there"

   "I understand"

   "You poor thing"

   "It never rains but it pours, doesn't it?"

   "You will be in our thoughts and prayers"

What you say, of course, is not important. It's your ability to make others who are beside themselves feel comfortable in the absence of content that really matters.

Good, Solid Chats

This is what we've been having. Tough, stern, but fair.

Notice the concern for your welfare. The understanding of your shortcomings to date, coupled with the sense of urgency in helping you to change your ways.

Soon you will be ready to do the same with a pitiably hip protégé of your own.

You will also need plenty of:

Toasts Suitable for Prayer Breakfasts

One day soon you may be invited to a 7:00 A.M. gathering of Establishment members who all sit down in their pinstripes with vest-pocket watch chains clattering against the breakfast table, say the Lord's Prayer together, then turn to you for a morning toast. You pick up your tiny orange juice glass out of the crushed ice in the little chrome hotel bowl and . . . what will you say?

Some recommendations:

Profound Toasts

The cure of crime is not the electric chair, but the high chair.

—J. Edgar Hoover

Democracy is nothing but an attempt to apply the principles of the Bible to a human society.

—Wallace C. Speers

"Had Abraham Lincoln been living today, the Rotary Club would supply him with a set of books; the Lions Club with a good reading lamp; the Cosmopolitan Club with writing equipment; and the Kiwanis Club with a wooden terrazzo for the cabin.

"He would have the protection of child labor insurance. A kindly philanthropist would send him to college with a scholarship.

"Incidentally, a case worker would see that his father received a monthly check from the county. He would receive a subsidy for rail splitting, another one for raising a crop he was going to raise anyway, and still another subsidy for not raising a crop he had no intention of raising.

"Result: There would have been no Abraham Lincoln!"

—Herbert V. Prochnow, *The Complete Toastmaster* (Englewood Cliffs, N.J.: Prentice-Hall, 1960), pp. 221–222.

Lighthearted Toasts

Let's lift a toast to a great clergyman—someone who seems to think the eternal gospel requires an everlasting sermon!

Let's lift a toast to a man who fought with the Marines—he couldn't get along with anybody!

> —Elmer Pastar, *Complete Book of Toasts, Boasts and Roasts* (West Nyack, N.Y.: Parker, 1982), p. 67.

And when the President of Sony Corporation is the guest of honor:

I break my bones before you.

> Which is Japanese, and refers to the severest form of genuflection.
> —Paul Dickson, *Toasts* (New York: Delacorte, 1981), p. 295.

My, but you're shaping up very nicely! Good show!

And you thought you wouldn't have the pluck to stick with it!

Now, let's move on to the next step of achieving moral superiority over the great majority of your peers.

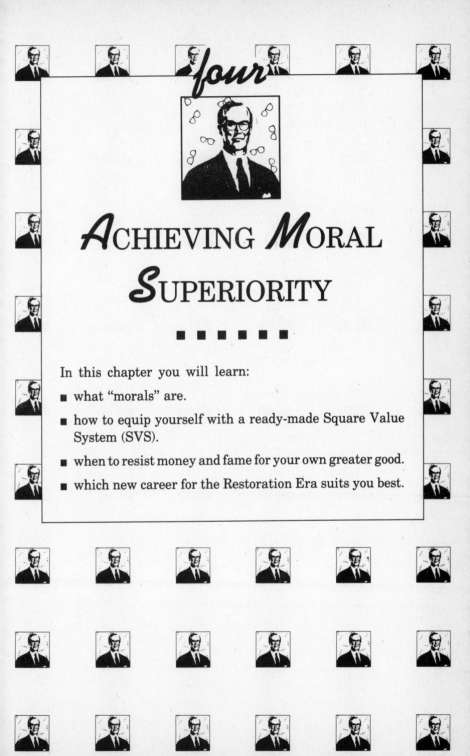

four

*A*CHIEVING *M*ORAL *S*UPERIORITY

■ ■ ■ ■ ■ ■

In this chapter you will learn:

■ what "morals" are.

■ how to equip yourself with a ready-made Square Value System (SVS).

■ when to resist money and fame for your own greater good.

■ which new career for the Restoration Era suits you best.

*M*orals. MOR-ALS. You try saying it once.

Now, our hair didn't all fall out at once, did it?

You can become just as comfortable with MOR-ALS as a system to live by. We'll sugar-coat them for you a bit, just the way you've been taught all your "hip" notions, by defining MOR-ALS as:

The science of how man is to conduct himself so that the story of his life may have a happy ending.
—Etienne Gilson,
Moral Values and The Moral Life

A happy ending! Isn't that what you enjoy most? Poor Uncle Etienne spent his *whole life* studying morals, and you can learn practically everything he did just by studying this short chapter!

Then, with your new Square Value System, you can take a pitying new look at all your old friends who meander through life like flotsam, doing just what they feel like, while you conduct yourself according to what you *know* is right.

MORALS: THE SQUARE SCIENCE

The ancient Greeks were a tempestuous lot, much more akin to the modern-day variety than you may imagine.

Their harmonious white buildings shown in all your schoolbooks undoubtedly had you visualizing a whole nation full of the white-cushioned, ivory-tiled homes shown in *Architectural Digest*, with tasteful and clearheaded occupants to match. In fact, the ravages of time bleached those buildings white. In 3000 B.C. they were painted red, yellow, blue, and may each have had a set of golden arches, for all we know.

Yet, the grandfather of modern squaredom emerged from the Athenian honky-tonk: Plato.

Plato, single-handedly (and modestly giving credit for his ideas to Socrates) advanced (1) a code of absolute morality, (2) government by a few of the most virtuous, and (3) censorship for the young to prevent them from learning bad habits.

In his *Republic* Plato courageously rebuked the original Yuppie, Thrasynochus, who claimed that "good is what I want." Plato patiently outlined a code of conduct making each person responsible for others and defining the First Establishment Doctrine: To establish and maintain the social order.

Because Plato was the first who dared to be square, he was rudely shouted down by "hip" Greek philosophers such as Aristotle, who adopted the rabble-pleasing theory that achieving happiness was more important than achieving virtue!

Aristotle excused the young from lectures on morality because they were too busy "pursuing passions"! Such lectures included the "doctrine of pleasure" and other permissivist claptrap hastily scrawled in his mass-market paperback *Ethics*.

Perhaps John Stuart Mill best summarized the difference between good morals (Plato's) and bad (Aristotle's) when he pointed out that he would rather be an unhappy Socrates than a happy pig.

Moral Wrap-up

So you do not become frustrated with the equivocating of different philosophers, here are the condensed teachings of the important moralists:

Moralist	Moral is:	Immoral is:
St. Thomas Aquinas	Whatever God says	Whatever God says
Spinoza	What works	What doesn't
John Stuart Mill	Whatever makes everybody happy	Whatever doesn't
Nietzsche	For smart people to decide	John Stuart Mill
Kant	Doing your duty	Doing your duty for selfish reasons
Hobbes	What the king says	What nature says

Can't agree on much of anything, can they? It will be more instructive to move directly to the guiding philosophers of the American Establishment, the Puritan divines Increase and Cotton Mather.

WHAT THE MATHERS SAY

	Moral is:	*Immoral is:*
Increase and Cotton Mather say:	Industry	Vanity
	Piety	Thievery
	Honesty	Lechery
	Humility	Treachery
	Decency	Adultery
	Loyalty	Witchery
	Simplicity	Bitchery
	Fidelity	Buggery
	Reliability	Thuggery
Jerry Mathers (as the Beaver) says:	Wally	Eddie

Now we're ready to construct a system of traditional morality that's right for you.

An Instant Square Values System
(SVS)
to Call Your Own

Even though you may never have owned or actually used a values system before, you will find that your Square Values System provides you with the right attitudes and behavior to apply in any circumstance or moral dilemma.

Good American Values
vs.
Bad Foreign Values

While we must be tolerant of those who hail from other lands, one cannot argue convincingly that foreign (i.e., "European" or "Asian") values hold a candle to good, solid American Establishment values.

Let's look at the record.

1. What nationality is Dr. Norman Vincent Peale, author of *The Power of Positive Thinking*?
   American _____   European _____   Asian _____

2. Who owns the Statue of Liberty?
   The U.S.A. _____   Europe _____   Asia _____

3. Who won the Revolutionary War?
   The U.S.A. _____   Europe _____   Asia _____

There can be no doubt that our core American values have earned the U.S.A. a piece of moral real estate unique in all the world. Thus the outer boundaries of a personal values system must embody what is right about America and eschew what is wrong about everywhere else.

Good American Values	Bad Foreign Values
Optimism ("Let's look to the future!")	**Pessimism** ("Let's wallow in the past!")
Can Do ("Let's get together and solve the problem!")	**Fatalism** ("Let's discuss why some problems can't be solved.")
Hard Work ("Let's roll up our sleeves and get started.")	**Passivism** ("Let's roll up our sleeves and get on the free drugs.")
Fair Play ("Everybody wins!")	**Cynicism** ("What will the ruling class do to us next?")
Capitalism ("Anybody can wind up in the money!")	**Socialism** ("Everybody can wind up on the dole.")

Even in a chaotic and threatening world, the core American values will always emerge triumphant.

■ ■ ■ ■ ■

SELFLESS INTERESTS: GIVE UNTIL IT HURTS

The Me Decade wasn't about you at all, was it?

Well, let's see for ourselves by answering a few simple questions:

1. Last holiday season I was busy:
    a. Cooking one hundred turkeys for my church group.

    b. Donating all my clothes to Goodwill Industries.
    c. Giving my holiday bonus and my new car to the United Way.

2. For my last birthday, I:
    a. Visited sick people at the hospital to hand them my birthday presents.
    b. Used my home as a shelter for the homeless.
    c. Gave my life savings to my parents to thank them for bringing me into the world.

3. If I had only one wish that would come true, it would be to:
    a. Bring Ike back to life so we can keep the world safe for democracy and have prosperity at home.
    b. Buy a new organ for the church.
    c. Secure the school principal a much deserved raise.

How did we do? If you answered "a, b, and c!" to each of them, you may skip this section. Any fewer correct answers, and a word to the wise will be necessary:

Grow up! You are not the center of the universe! The rest of us are not here for your convenience and amusement! We expect you to do more than your duty, because just about everyone else is more important than you are!

Give until it hurts like a hundred broken bones, then give some more! You may no longer judge your life by the transient pleasures you give yourself, but by the happiness you bring others!

Did you make each family member's life a little better today? Did you pray together to stay together? Were you true to your school? What did you donate to your church? Did you send your $16 a month to save a child? Did you give blood (not sell it) to the Red Cross?

Don't try to read any further until you do all the above, and more.

We're waiting.

Ah, you're back. Didn't that give you a warm glow of satisfaction? One that you can feel anytime you sacrifice your own selfish interests to make someone happy?

A Personal Code of Behavior: 41 Commandments for Today

Moses was quite right, of course. But he did not go far enough. The Ten Commandments have, over time, been read as liberally as federal judges misinterpret the Constitution!

To behave with moral certainty, it will be necessary for you to memorize all 41 commandments entered here and live by them scrupulously.

Sorry if you were expecting a burning bush.

1. Thou shalt not read *Playboy*'s special on "The Girls of the Episcopal Church."

2. Thou shalt not cook Cajun or use cayenne peppers.

3. Thou shalt not dance except for the box step and, of course, square dancing.

4. Thou shalt not watch "Saturday Night Live," except for the Church Lady.

5. That shalt not wear anything sold in Victoria's Secret.

6. Thou shalt not have a car phone.

7. Thou shalt not appear in any newspaper except *The New York Times* upon your birth and death.

8. Thou shalt not shop in The Sharper Image or Banana Republic.

9. Thou shalt not buy any foreign car.

10. Thou shalt not sleep naked.

11. Thou shalt not buy greeting cards that pop up to reveal Coney Island.

12. Thou shalt not wear dinner jackets with blue ruffled shirts.

13. Thou shalt not listen to Madonna or Twisted Sister.

14. Thou shalt not visit drive-in churches.

15. Thou shalt not ever visit Las Vegas or Atlantic City.

16. Thou shalt not covet thy neighbor's wife's boyfriend.

17. Thou shalt not eat Ben & Jerry's Brownie Bars.

18. Thou shalt not watch MTV.

19. Thou shalt not watch.

20. Thou shalt not take any drug but aspirin, and then only for a heart attack.

21. Thou shalt not have your teeth bonded.

22. Thou shalt not read Hite reports.

23. Thou shalt not discuss thy income.

24. Thou shalt not kill time in video arcades.

25. Thou shalt not know who Robert Longo or Mary Boone is.

26. Thou shalt not complain of PMS.

27. Thou shalt not attend any musical produced after 1960.

28. Thou shalt not place personal ads.

29. Thou shalt not wear Porsche sunglasses.

30. Thou shalt not buy hand-painted ties that say "Kiss Me, Baby."

31. Thou shalt not buy on margin.

32. Thou shalt not raise Yuppie Puppies.

33. Thou shalt not brush-kiss in greeting.

34. Thou shalt not say *"Ciao"* in parting.

35. Thou shalt not wear male underwear that says "Home of the Whopper."

36. Thou shalt not carry a beeper.

37. Thou shalt not talk to thy neighbors in the movies.

38. Thou shalt not giggle in church.

39. Thou shalt not do one minute managing.

40. Thou shalt not read trendy books.

41. Thou shalt not worry about bottom lines.

And don't even think about looking for legalistic loopholes to squeak some improper attitude or behavior through. You are being watched every minute to make certain that you comply with the spirit as well as the letter of the 41 Commandments.

Now we're ready for a good moral workout!

OPERATING YOUR NEW VALUE SYSTEM

If you have ever been able to follow the instructions for hooking up a hip new stereo system, you will be able to follow the directions provided here for plugging in your new Square Value System.

MORAL WIRING CHART:
HOW TO OPERATE YOUR NEW
SQUARE VALUES SYSTEM (SVS)

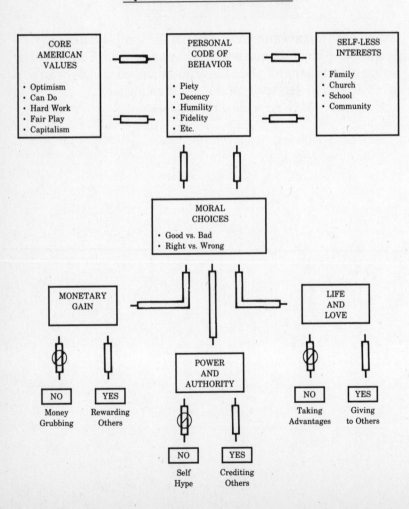

The test of whether you have mastered the wiring will be to see how well you can cope with common moral dilemmas of the modern age.

Ready? Here we go.

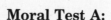

Moral Test A:

*O*PPORTUNITIES FOR *E*GREGIOUS *S*ELF-*H*YPE

1. Your college lecture notes for Political Science 101 seem to have wandered their way into one of Joe Biden's speeches as he campaigns for Sheriff of Knot's Landing, California. You decide to:
   a. Call Michael Dukakis's staff to publicize the event nationally for you.
   b. Call Joe Biden's staff to correct his misunderstanding of your notes by proclaiming in his speeches that the first U.S. President was General Cornwallis.

2. Many years ago your mother sent your childhood drawings, without your knowledge, to the Curator of the Smithsonian. Through a routine delay in U.S. postal delivery, they arrived only yesterday. The curator wants to make them the subject of a special exhibition. You ask her:
   a. To see whether you can get a PBS tie-in special.
   b. To see whether there isn't a more deserving child artist somewhere in the world.

3. Your virtuous life is noticed by Merv Griffin, who wants to turn it into a pilot for a game show called "The Fly-Over Squares." You respond by:
   a. Signing with an agent.

b. Signing a contract in which you modestly demand that your name will appear nowhere in the credits as a creative consultant or executive producer.

■ ■ ■ ■ ■ ■

▪ ▪ ▪ ▪ ▪

Moral Test B:

OPPORTUNITIES FOR OFFENSIVE MONEY-GRUBBING

1. You have staged such a successful church fund-raising drive in your community that a California entrepreneur wants to franchise your methods for Biblical Encyclopedia sales. He offers you $1 million cash. You advise him:

    a. To hand-deliver your check to account #3649, Bank of the Bahamas, anonymously.

    b. To hand-deliver your check to The American Heart Association, anonymously.

2. The child you sponsor in Central America for $16 a month has been approached by a toy company to be the commercial spokesperson for the Contra Doll. You tell the company:

    a. You have her signature on a personal management agreement and demand a $300,000 per year contract.

    b. You have her best interest at heart and will let her sell the Contra Doll for nothing because it's the patriotic thing to do.

3. Aggressive divorce attorney Marvin Mitchelson likes you a lot, but just hates your filthy-rich wife or husband. You tell him you want to:

    a. Sue her/him for $10 million on grounds of incompatibility at duplicate bridge.

    b. Sue Merv Griffin for $1 for blurting your name out during a show as a "wonderful human being," breaking your pact of modesty.

▪ ▪ ▪ ▪ ▪

■ ■ ■ ■ ■ ■

Moral Test C:

OPPORTUNITIES TO TAKE UNFAIR ADVANTAGE

1. You live next door to a special home for members of the opposite sex who suffer from extremely low intelligence, coupled with unbelievable physical beauty. You go visiting next door to:
   a. Bring them a welcome wagon kit full of items which you purchased at the Pink Pussycat Boutique.
   b. Bring them a special education videotape on Celibacy Made Simple.

2. You have an elderly relative who will celebrate her ninetieth birthday soon, has amassed a fortune of more than $1 billion dollars, and is well known to hear imaginary voices. You drop by to:
   a. Spell out the terms of her new will from behind the curtains.
   b. Spell out her legal right to, if she desires, leave all her money to her favorite character on "All My Children."

3. As a research scientist, you are blessed with a terribly hard-working but modest assistant at the laboratory where you work. She has just left on your desk a formula outlining a cure for the common cold she has been developing. It works. You:
   a. Thank her for her "notes" and sign your own name on the "Patent Owner" line before passing it on to the Nobel committee.
   b. Thank her for her contribution to humankind and concentrate on your own life's work of placing miniature Bibles in Roach Motels.

■ ■ ■ ■ ■ ■

TEST ANSWERS

If you don't absolutely *know* what's right without being told, you have left a wire loose somewhere.

If you're feeling a comfortable new rigidity about your beliefs, congratulations! These, like arteries, will continue to harden as you grow older.

Now that you're ready to saddle up and save weaker souls with good works, just what is it that you do for a living?

Won't it be just slightly difficult to pursue a career grooming Akitas in Beverly Hills when what you really want to do is pull those Lamborghini Countach drivers out of their cars and point out how spiritually impoverished their lives are? Not to worry.

MORALLY SUPERIOR CAREER CHANGES FOR THE RESTORATION ERA

Few professions that drew envious squeals during the 1970s and early 1980s will pass muster under the closer moral scrutiny of the Restoration Era. While it will be considered impolite to sneer visibly at, say, a rock musician in the 1990s, you will no longer see them lurching onto the Johnny Carson show either, anymore than you would expect the organist to break into a U2 medley at church!

Moving to your own career choice, made during a time of cultural narcissism and reflecting on obsession with selfish gain, we will need to embark upon some hasty career counseling to prepare you for the Restoration Era with a calling better suited to your new improved morality.

*T*HE 7 *B*EST *C*AREER *C*HANGES FOR THE *1990s*

From Pitiably Hip	To Profitably Square
1. Advertising Executive	1. Vicar
2. Actor	2. CIA Operative
3. Yuppie Stockbroker	3. Corporate Ethics Adviser
4. Dope Lawyer	4. Back to Prosecutor
5. *Rolling Stone* Writer	5. Religious Publisher
6. Fashion Designer	6. Uniform Designer
7. "Get Rich Watching TV" Seminar Leader	7. "Dare to Be Square" Seminar Leader

From Advertising Executive ...

We've seen you pirouetting on your feet, flashing that sincere smile, weaving a spell to convince some soft-drink manufacturer to pay for those sexy little ditties full of new-wave camera angles and bronzed, angular models with freezed-up hair and Brazilian thong bathing suits.

Only $50,000,000 of the clients' money and oh, what a star you were at the award shows! Stepping up to receive your Clio awards with the best of them!

You lowered your eyes modestly, fondling the little gold statuette, and spun a modest tale of how advertising is really a collaborative business. But we knew you really did it all by yourself. Your idea! Your words! Your images! You showed the models how to smile! The camera people how to point! The sun how to set!

You were the toast of Madison Avenue and fluttered pulses everywhere.

Of course, then the people who ran your agency decided they'd put in thirty or so hard years, and wouldn't it be a good idea to merge with another agency so they could retire fat as hogs.

The Big Bang! And in the fallout you slipped through a crack without benefit of a golden parachute.

What to do with one so clever, so creative, such a delightful raconteur, welcome anywhere for your wry humor and sincerity.

What lateral move could be more Noel Coward-ly than . . .

To Vicar!

A few good hard years of repentance, theological study, and celibacy, and you're off on a new career as Suburban Churchman!

You'll arrive at a quaint New Establishment village somewhere in Connecticut, lined with genteel eighteenth-century houses around the common and, on the horizon, a glorious country church with a steeple to the sky!

Now you can join the gentry for cocktails on the terrace, sipping your martinis gently, please, and the opportunity to regale your well-padded flock with the acquired wit and gentle wisdom of a genuine Anglican vicar.

Now, instead of having to spend your time quipping away with art directors in those little offices full of toy Japanese robot collections, you can project your true depth and character as you amuse one and all with clever turns of phrase. But now they have to laugh! It's a captive audience! Unlike those advertising clients who make frosted flakes out in the Midwest somewhere and would not chuckle if you yanked off their shoes and tickled their feet, nobody is ever rude to a vicar.

From Actor . . .

Worse yet, you may have sweated away the seventies and eighties in acting courses, struggling to emote, then vying with less talented practitioners of your craft at miserable auditions (cattle calls) where your fate rested in the hands of mindless dolts or patently envious fools.

But then, once in a great while, the pure brilliance of your performance would burn like a white light unto the souls of all present, and you had a Job. So what if it was the Poconos Dinner Theater with tourists banging their silverware and shouting across their tables to spouses with hearing aids? Nobody ever made a walk-on in *The King and I* light up the sky as you did!

What could be more gratifying at twenty-one? Or more humiliating after thirty?

It's time to quit your day job at Western Union doing singing telegrams dressed as a giant pizza and sharpen your talents for a patriotic move . . .

To CIA Operative!

The CIA is looking for a few good men and women who are U.S. born, with a facility for languages.

That, of course, just scratches the surface of their actual hiring agenda.

To impress your CIA interviewer, come in disguise. Wear an acrylic wig, a phony moustache, and a mouth device between lip and gums to cloak your natural voice.

Also, learn the correct responses to questions raised in a CIA interview:

Q: So, tell me about yourself.

A: No.

Q: Do you like dealing with assets . . . er . . . people?

A: Only with extreme prejudice.

Q: Do you enjoy foreign travel?

A: I always wanted to see Afghanistan.

And all the while concentrate on your remarkable qualifications for your new role.

You love to play at being someone you are not.

You experience no shame in admitting you will do anything to get the part.

You have already conquered your stagefright. Now you only need to practice lying down under a few speeding trains to control your apprehensions about a sudden, hideous death.

You could be the next William J. Casey, subject (albeit posthumously) of a #1 best-seller!

Break a leg.

From Yuppie Stockbroker...

Where were you on October 8, 1987?

Selling short, or slamming your clients into longer and stronger runs with the stampeding bull market?

The intoxicating scent of naked greed! The leap to stardom! And then the heart-clutching plunge to obscurity after Black Monday.

Perhaps you suffered the cruelties of the immediate aftermath. ("What's the difference between a Yuppie stockbroker and a pigeon? A pigeon can still make a deposit on a BMW.") The headwaiters who took to laughing at your threadbare suit, where they used to bow and scrape at your arrival. Trying to break your five-year contract at the athletic club. Whimpering for bridge loans at the bank where you were once courted, but are now despised, to meet the whopping balloon payment on your condo.

Stop your sniffling. It's only money.

Besides, you acquired some eminently useful skills over an entire career dedicated to manipulating others' childish dreams of getting something for nothing. You clearly understood the difference between right and wrong, and unfailingly chose the latter. What better way to rehabilitate yourself than making the common-sense move...

To Corporate Ethics Adviser!

Lease yourself a good Brooks Brothers suit, hang up a colonial shingle in an appropriate college town, and you're back in business.

Fortune 500 companies desperately need your hands-on experience to counsel their executives and employees on how to conduct ethical "good business" in the post-crash morality of the nineties.

Where fangs out, let-'em-eat-cake, short-term tactics were the sexy management characteristics of the eighties, in the nineties the watchword is safe sex. Abiding values. Sound, managed growth. No funny business about insider trading, winking at antitrust legislation, letting their employees bribe middle management to buy their jumbo jets instead of Boeings, or dumping their toxic waste in the city reservoir.

And don't be timid about imposing the strict moral code of business behavior so notably lacking in your former life. They need and demand a vicious tongue-lashing from CEO on down to repair the moral decay it took so many years of selfish interest to accomplish.

Now get in front of the mirror and practice your gravest possible expressions. Buy a gold watch with a chain to pull out of your vest pocket and exclaim, "We have precious little time and a great deal of healing to be done here," no matter what the appearance of corporate compliance might be. Everybody has something to hide after lounging in the moral hot tub of business practice in the seventies and eighties.

From Dope Lawyer . . .

Well, we were certainly in the right place at the right time, weren't we?

Graduating from University of Miami law school in 1980, just in time for the wave of Colombian dopers who poured billions of dollars through South Florida banks, and rednecks from the Everglades who checked out in DC-3s and went for "square grouper" in their charter fishing boats.

A year in the Federal Prosecutor's office and you were ready for private practice.

You bought an AMG Mercedes with ground effects, like an expensive low rider, and windows blackened so nobody could see in. Perhaps you even had a sleek Lear 35A to cart your cash retainers down to Panama.

Except then the DEA, Special Task Force, and IRS froze all

your clients' liquid assets to prevent them from hiring effective counsel, and where did that leave you?

Ready to take that Robert Hall suit, J. C. Penney shirt, and dime-store tie out of your closet and return to those thrilling days of yesteryear . . .

Back to Prosecutor!

Where there's smoke there's fire! If they didn't do anything wrong, why did they get arrested in the first place? Now get out there and fight! Suspend habeas corpus. Push for martial law south of Palm Beach.

Here's the profile it's supposed to be "unconstitutional" to use, but will enable you to sniff out a doper, just like a trained German shepherd, at any shopping mall.

Age: 19
Sex: Male
Occupation: None
Income: $10,000,000 per year
Clothing: Armani, Versace, Ferre
Automobile: Ferrari 308GT, Mercedes 500 SEL
Distinguishing Marks: Santeria Tattoos
Distinguishing Behavior: Lights candles, then strangles chickens

You have a whole gallery of the guilty right in your old law partner's waiting room.

Don't you know there's a war on?

From Rolling Stone *Writer . . .*

The movie *Perfect* was really about you, wasn't it?

You apprenticed with Dr. Hunter S. Thompson somewhere in Mexico. The two of you found a dental supply house nearby to buy plenty of nitrous oxide tanks, and busloads of German tourists to amuse you with stories of coyote sightings and having all their clothes stolen.

You cut your teeth on investigative journalism, exposing the management of CBS as the power behind a huge communications conglomerate, catching an urban mayor in the act of accepting campaign contributions, and breaking the story that one of the major bands of '81 made it to the top of the charts by playing music designed to get airplay on teenage stations.

You would have won a Pulitzer in '82 for your painstakingly documented revelation of academic politics at Harvard if the committee hadn't felt sorry for the other reporter who lost her hand covering an Iranian religious service.

Then the magazine that used to offer a free roach clip to each new subscriber started covering issues of interest to that greedy pig moving through the demographic python, the aging Baby Boomer.

Focus groups to decide what stories to write! Drug testing for employees! Advertisers like the U.S. Army looking for recruits! And you're ... fired for general irrelevance and a bad testing lab report!

Never trust a magazine over twenty! Better clean out your desk and make the shrewd career move ...

To Religious Publisher . . .

Not religious, you say? Neither was Chuck Colson, the Watergate conspirator who wanted to firebomb the Brookings Institute, and once said that he would walk over his own grandmother to see Richard Nixon reelected President! (When in doubt, look to the Watergate crowd and you'll find bizarre precedents for anything.)

Today Colson makes his living as an inspirational writer and lecturer, who churns out books and videos with the same old steam he once used to roll over his opponents. His good works include "The Myth of the Money Tree" and "Dear Pat Robertson: Winning isn't Everything" in *Christianity Today,* and *Loving God.*

Why not you? Thanks to the opportunities available through desktop publishing, you can set up shop, like Chuck, right in your prison cell if need be.

Some creative ideas for articles:

- ▪ "Jann Wenner: Hell-Bound Hipster or Son of Satan?"
- ▪ "The Pulitzer Prize Committee: Coven or Cabal?"
- ▪ "The Baby Boomers: Brainless Bed of Kelp or Captive Cult?"
- ▪ "Drug Testers: Communist Conspiracy or Atheistic Assassination Squad?"

Buy yourself a direct-mail list of people who subscribe to the *National Enquirer,* merge it with a list of people who've bought Bibles recently, and you've got a market bigger than *Rolling Stone* will ever be!

From Fashion Designer ...

How you made them react with slimy green envy when you unveiled the late seventies Retro look in ... 1980! Fifteen—no, twenty—years ahead of your time.

And the beauty of it was, you only had to Xerox those recent issues of *W* and *GQ* to put a whole portfolio together, then buy out last spring's returns to put on the racks for fall.

How were you supposed to predict the hip hysteria for animal skins when that dumb movie *Clan of the Cave Bear IV* came out?

What a sweet irony that, in the Restoration Era, you'll be sitting pretty with the squarest career of all when you make your move to ...

Uniform Designer: The Hot Creative Career for the Nineties

Now that practically all America wants to show up in uniform, how could we abide those ill-fitting, khaki-drab wonders the U.S. Army got its people up in before chevrons became chic?

Then came the $50 million appropriation to Fashion Institute of Technology and L.A. Art Center to redress the fashion grievances of a whole century of uniforms only a civilian on the job for two years would put up with.

To help you create the sense of style so notably lacking in those with a sense of duty, we may hark back to the glorious years of clothes-savvy combat, the nineteenth century. When Fashion Avenue wasn't in Paris or Milan, but Prussia.

Some research to set your imagination free in the right direction:

> *In typical hussar fashion, the Prussian hussars changed their head-dress with remarkable frequency adopting the mirliton or flugelmutz, the shako in various forms and returning towards the middle of the nineteenth century to the original hussar-styled head-dress: the busby. Prints of the Prussian army of the 1940s show the hussar with a tall cylindrical fur-covered busby with oval cockade in white and black at the top front holding a white plume, and a coloured bag falling to the left.*
>
> —R. J. Wilkinson-Lathan, *Collecting Militaria* (New York: Arco, 1975), pp. 68–69.

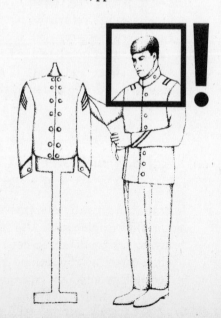

The Prussian Cavalry, c. 1843, showing the various uniforms of each unit.

From "Get Rich Watching TV" Seminar Leader . . .

You were one of the first to buy into those one-hour commercials (did anybody really think they were regular programs?) on how to get rich in America during the superheated greedy spell of the mid 1980s.

And what a concept you brought to America's more desperate living rooms! You began with the obligatory germ of reality, the fact that some people make money in real estate. Then you developed a program just for people who considered themselves Lifetime Losers, but could muster enough business acumen to apply for a bank credit card and packaged "How to Build a Real Estate Empire with Plastic!"

Your game plan, as you explained carefully on a blackboard in front of a huge audience, tastefully attired in your *Saturday Night Fever* white disco suit, was simple:

1. Blast your credit card to its max and put down $5,000 on an FHA home in a dismal but not totally bombed-out neighborhood.
2. Find quiet, neat, fussy tenants, like a retired gay couple.
3. Sell the home after five years.
4. Do it again four hundred or five hundred times and you'll be rich!

Nobody got hurt; in fact they were able to buy your leatherette-bound loose-leaf binders chock full of information for only $395 by calling the toll-free number, to display on their coffee tables. And you got rich! In America!

Of course, the authorities came down a little hard on you after that tiny "guarantee" claim you didn't think anybody would take too seriously, and after you paid all your fines, you were able to move into one of those FHA homes yourself and scrape enough cash together for a half-priced drink at Happy Hour on Friday evenings.

But, as the saying goes, if you have what it takes to make it once, you can make it twice. So get ready to move . . .

To "Dare to Be Square" Seminar Leader!

Just send $395 now and we'll rush you the complete Square System with all you need to offer Dare to Be Square Seminars in your own home!

You'll find:

(1) A loose-leaf binder with the pages of this book enlarged to 8½" × 11" and three convenient holes punched in each page.
(2) An audio tape with all the information in this book prerecorded for listening in the privacy of your Mercury Comet.
(3) A Mobil map of your city, showing many streets which undoubtedly house locations where Square Seminars might be offered.

And when you act now, we'll include a FREE slide presentation depicting all the photographs and illustrations in this book, in high-contrast black and white . . .

*H*A! *G*OTCHA! *T*HIS *W*AS THE *F*INAL *T*EST OF *Y*OUR *N*EW *S*QUARE *V*ALUES *S*YSTEM!

Do you really think the New Establishment stoops to that sorry predatory behavior?

This is a serious discussion of morality. You should be ashamed of yourself for slipping back into your old get-rich fantasies. Now what are we going to do with you?

Better write the 41 Commandments on your blackboard one hundred times and take an icy cold shower for good measure.

Then report back here to ponder the wealth of other career changes you can look forward to in the years ahead.

From:	*To:*
8. I.R.S.-listed "Problem" Accountant	8. I.R.S. Collection Agent
9. Rock Musician	9. Dean of Conservatory
10. Sex Education Teacher	10. Consultant on Permissible School Prayer
11. Hip Sculptor	11. Taxidermist Specializing in Owls
12. Offshore Banker	12. African Missionary

From:	To:
13. Cosmetic Surgeon	13. Christian Science Practitioner
14. Aerobics Instructor	14. Scouting Troop Leader
15. Trendy College Professor	15. Dorm Mother
16. Publicist	16. Anonymist
17. Videographer	17. Librarian
18. Dancer	18. Fencing Instructor
19. Prancer	19. Permanent Fixture
20. Vixen	20. Housewife

Your options are limited only by a grown-up lack of imagination.

And once you've settled comfortably into employment, you can turn to the glorious pursuit of square love!

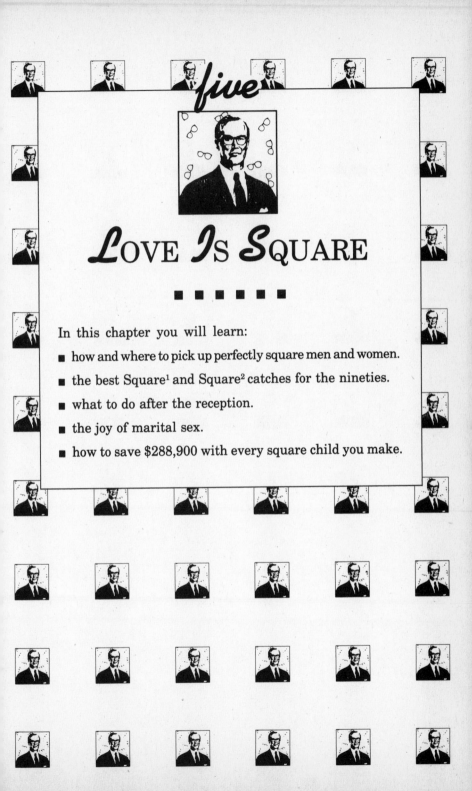

five

LOVE IS SQUARE

∎ ∎ ∎ ∎ ∎ ∎

In this chapter you will learn:

- how and where to pick up perfectly square men and women.
- the best Square[1] and Square[2] catches for the nineties.
- what to do after the reception.
- the joy of marital sex.
- how to save $288,900 with every square child you make.

*A*nd how is *your* love life these days? If you're single, perhaps you've pulled in the horns a bit, so to speak, given the dangers stalking the current sexual landscape. But cheer up! No need to worry about those thrilling moments of yesteryear spent writhing in ignorant passion, glistening with scented body oil on a water bed with satin sheets, lucky if you knew your partner's first name, let alone sexual history.

Just consider yourself fortunate to be alive in the Restoration Era, now that courtly love will once again flower across the land! Sweet, old-fashioned ballads on the phonograph! Front-porch swings that squeak! Marriages arranged by parents!

Because blissfully monogamous relationships sealed by the marital vows will be every responsible adult's dream, you will want to apply yourself diligently to wooing and winning your true love's hand. All you need is a carefully structured game plan, and no slip-ups, ever.

If you've already married, good show! Who says virtue goes unrewarded? Now your life's work may be dedicated to the joy of strictly marital sex and its functional purpose of making perfectly square children.

*H*OW *P*ORCUPINES *M*AKE *L*OVE: *S*INGLE *S*QUAREHOOD IN THE *1990s*

Let's take a good look at ourselves, shall we?

No, not down *there!* Face to face, in the mirror!

Be grateful that whatever you may see, a square mate will be

waiting patiently for you if you know where to look. You merely
need to know how to recognize your heart's desire. And what to
say, or not say, so you don't send your prospective loved one bolting
away like a skittish colt.

The following chart illustrates a scientific analysis of popular
romantic choices in the 1980s. You would do well to study it
carefully in order to avoid virtually all the personality types you
have grown accustomed to dating, and concentrate single-mindedly
on those you probably passed by without notice because they
happened to be wearing Argyle socks or incredibly unflattering
eyeglasses. Both of which will qualify as high-excitement pher-
omones for your new dating career.

POPULAR ROMANTIC CHOICES IN
THE LATE 1980s

MEN

YUP PUPS
Profile: Dan

Age: 26
Occupation: Popcorn Futures Broker
Last Book Read: *Bright Lights, Big City*
Quote: "You busy tonight?"

PETER PAN FLYWAYS
Profile: Alan

Age: 37
Occupation: Lionel Train Engineer
Last Book Read: *The Hardy Boys*
Quote: "I'll call you."

21   39

MTV AEROBICISTS
Profile: Patty

Age: 23
Occupation: Flight Attendant on promotional blimp
Last Book Cover Read: *Less Than Zero*
Quote: "I'm still waiting for the right Mercedes to come along."

HITE CASES
Profile: Susan

Age: 36
Occupation: Women's Attack Group Leader
Last Book Read: *No Good Men*
Quote: "Are you absolutely sure you're not married?"

WOMEN

Square Women, Foolish Choices

In this transitional period from the old hip-style relationships to new square ones, even bright, confident women who run huge institutions may need special guidance to steer clear of men who "seem" square enough at first blush, but turn out to be quite vomit-worthy when it's too late to do much of anything but think about suicide.

Some hints to help you smell three common rats by recognizing hidden danger signs:

Actor with Boyfriend

He may be great looking and a glib talker. He may tug at your maternal instincts with his self-pity and theft of your credit cards. But don't confuse his spoiled antics and live-in boyfriend for signs of a "square-in identity crisis."

Best Friend's Father

It's easy to fall for this smoothie. He may even convince you that you're only the first or second of his daughter's friends he's ever had an affair with, and that he'll leave your best friend's mother for you! Your best strategy: Tell him you'd love to join him alone in his study, then remark that it has an odor of old people about it.

A Federal Prisoner

In these days of white-collar prosecution, it's more likely than ever that you'll fall in love with a convicted felon, just because you replied to a promising personal ad from a man who said he would not even look at another woman until he heard from you, then listed a P.O. Box in Danbury, CT.

Now the problem seems to be that he's getting out soon, and although you would really like to pretend this never happened, he has your name, address, phone number, employer, and some personal things you said in your letters you'd rather not see revealed in public. Plus you've been getting some very strange hang-up calls lately, as well as the feeling that the same utility truck has been sitting in front of your house for two days. And at work, right now, there are two FBI-types talking earnestly to your boss, who obviously doesn't like what they're saying.

See what a problem falling for the wrong man can be?

Safe and Sound Choices

Now let's look at some of the desirable square-type males you'll want to concentrate on meeting in the nineties.

The Nice Young Man from a Good Family

This is the male type who has instantly repelled you from the time you were a teenager, strangely attracted to the wild, haunted young men with dirty fingernails and long juvenile court records who struck you as irrepressibly sexy, while your parents kept trotting out nice young men with well-scrubbed faces and matching tie and handkerchief sets.

But why did they make you recoil in such horror? Exactly! Because they practically screamed "Square" with each awkward turn of phrase! Now that your old boyfriends have died in 100-mile-per-hour police chases, those nice young men you spurned so cruelly may have acquired a certain luster. Time to drag out those high school and college yearbooks, find the boys voted least likely to become James Dean, and get a good private detective on the case of locating your new heartthrob from old photographs. Chances are, he's still sitting wondering what you're up to, listening to old favorites like "Love Letters in the Sand" on his hi-fi, single as ever. (Worst-case scenario: He has been married to, and was recently divorced by, a hip wife who left him just enough to buy you a milkshake on Friday night at the Woolworth's counter.)

The Square Bachelor-About-Town

Unlike the Peter Pan Flyaway single man of the 1980s, whose sexual conquests before checking out of relationships are matters of song and story, the square bachelor-about-town restricts himself to a few carefully selected dates, with whom he's likely to end the evening on a firm handshake or chaste kiss on the (closed) lips or cheek.

The square-about-town is usually the grown-up, urbane incarnation of a nice boy from a good family who went to an Ivy League school and learned about life. He remains a bachelor only because he can't seem to locate his life's partner, no matter how many dinners he attends as the sought-after single man. To his credit, this constant exposure to women, mostly hip in outlook and therefore dead wrong for him, lends our unconfirmed bachelor a social poise seldom if ever encountered in other square types.

Rather than wear sacklike clothes of little distinction, the square bachelor-about-town may sport good British wools and tweeds, with buttons on the sleeves that actually work. His role model, if any, is likely to be Prince Charles, although he has pledged to himself that he will hold out, unlike Charles, for a suitable bride and not just any virgin with a pretty face.

The Square-in-the-Rough

It remains a sad fact of life for the single square woman that she and her kind will continue to outnumber eligible square bachelors by a factor of 24 to 1. Thus, the odds of falling in love and marrying a perfectly square partner after thirty-five will be roughly equivalent to her likelihood of being seized by a giant ape in mid-Manhattan and squired to the top of the Empire State Building.

This means, for all practical purposes, that you may need to lower your sights a bit to find a delightfully square soul inside a package that may not meet your exact specifications.

Here are some common traits you'll find in the most gratifying discovery of all, the "Square-in-the-Rough":

1. *Never speaks.* Not for him the narcissistic, clever patter of your old boyfriends! He may happen to speak only when you are glancing away or searching the floor for your napkin, so you have the sense of a man who has never opened his mouth to you in greeting or conversation. Remember, though, still waters run deep!

2. *Understands no current cultural references.* If his eyes glaze over when you mention "L.A. Law," this should be considered the heartening sign of a man who spends his idle hours perusing old copies of *National Geographic* and will attend to you with the same seriousness of purpose. Bonus: He is probably also unaware of Monday Night Football.

3. *Adopts a highly nondescript personal style.* If his clothing has you guessing about the possible century of origin, he will never look silly in old photographs as the years go by.

4. *Sends you two dozen long-stemmed daisies at the office, with a sentimental Hallmark thank-you card.* Didn't he care enough to send the very best? What greater gift could any man give?

Best Catch, Male Under 30
THE SQUARE HEIR

ARTHUR DAVIS REED, JR.

Age: 22

Apparent Occupation: Vista Volunteer

Actual Occupation: Rich man's son

Avocation: Putting away childish things

Education: Small liberal arts college offering a classical education

Latest Accomplishment: Sailed his Morgan across New York Harbor and returned safely.

Last Book Read: William F. Buckley, Jr., *God & Man at Yale*

Favorite Haunts: Country clubs nobody's heard of

Fantasy Woman: Latest Star of Glamorous Ladies of Wrestling (G.L.O.W.)

Actually Looking for the Woman Who: Married dear old Dad, and is prepared to wait until an exact clone appears.

Best Catch, Male Over 30
*7*HE *D*EBONAIR *S*QUARE

WILLIAM "BILL" BILLINGS

Age: 40 +

Occupations: Senior Trust Officer, Bank

Avocations: Senior Member, Clubs and Boards
              Square Bachelor-About-Town

Education: Ivy League, seasoned by a responsible life

Latest Accomplishment: Not marrying wrong candidate #572, a Junior Editor of *Savvy*

Last Book Read: *Who Killed Society?*

Favorite Haunts: Union League Club, University Club, Athletic Club, Diners Club, Book-of-the-Month Club

Fantasy Woman: The Mayflower Madam

Actually Looking for the Woman Who: Knows instinctively to put his martini in the freezer precisely an hour before he gets home.

Men: How to Make Love to a Square Woman

The man of good character will need little instruction in finding and winning his square mate. All other men should listen up.

The whole world over, there are only two different types of square woman, both equally desirable for the long-term if not equally attractive at first glance.

Square[1] Type Female

The "simple" square type appears truly different from the women you know. Although she couldn't spot a Gianfranco Ferre suit in the middle of a J. C. Penney store, and may not be able to keep stray hairs out of her mouth on a date, she possesses a generous heart overflowing with adoration for the man of her rather unimaginative dreams. She loves horses, dogs, furry little woodland creatures, and all other forms of sublimated maternal and sexual desire. She waits patiently to transfer it all to you.

So don't be put off by her knotty sweaters and funny rounded collars, her knee socks and flannel skirts, the shapeless haircut and oversized glasses that slip down her nose. This is a woman who knows how to give and forgive.

You need only be gentle, kind, and pleasantly persistent as her many layers of shyness are stripped away to reveal a soul of depth and, yes, passion.

Square² Type Female

The "complex" square type may look like a preppie, or a businesswoman who dresses in the traditional flannel bag and blouse-with-executive-sized-bow favored by female IBM sales representatives, or a Sheila E. look-alike for all you know.

But her distinguishing characteristic, apparent only through observation and close interrogation, is a soul in torment. When her friends drag her to Chippendale's and drunkenly slip twenty-dollar bills into the male strippers' underwear, she is the one left sitting dejectedly at the table, blushing, eyes averted, wishing she were home looking up old boyfriends in her high school yearbook.

She may be the college date you had to work up the nerve to ask out because you were convinced that her dark eye shadow hinted at raw desire, when they really concealed an excruciating desire to be anything but what she really was: shamefully square.

Naturally, Square¹ and Square² types require a somewhat different initiative to make the love connection. For example:

THE 10 BEST OPENING LINES

Square¹ Type Woman

Square² Type Woman

At the Supermarket

1. I'm just reminded that I have two tickets to the Land O'Lakes Butter factory tour. Would you care to join me?

1. Do you think it's true about subliminal advertising? I believe the tiger on that cereal box just winked at you.

At the Art Museum

2. I admire all paintings of children, but I love Keene best.

2. Call me a prude, but I think modern artists use too much red.

Square¹ Type Woman	*Square² Type Woman*

At the Library

3. Say, could you tell me where to find *All Creatures Great and Small*?

3. Pardon, but you seem to have checked out the only *Miss Manners*. May I ask you a brief question about White House invitations?

At the Class Reunion

4. I always stood outside the Glee Club just to hear you sing.

4. I still think about you every time I see Diane on "Cheers."

At the Church Dance

5. I don't think I've ever seen such a pretty gingham dress.

5. Would you keep me in mind for the next Peabody?

At the Post Office

6. I couldn't help noticing that you use Snoopy stationery too.

6. Not that it's any of my business, but I think you'll find a bad element if you become a member of public TV.

On Vacation

7. I've always wondered how you Amish feel about that Shaker furniture.

7. I think it's wrong to gamble even in international waters. Perhaps a walk on deck instead?

Square¹ Type Woman	*Square² Type Woman*

In the Doctor's Waiting Room

8. It's just a scratch really, and a small price to pay for saving a puppy from being run over by a speeding car.

8. I've always wondered what blood test results look like. Could I see yours?

In the Hottest After-Hours Club

9. Pardon, but I noticed that your date left an hour ago.

9. What's a nice girl/woman like you doing in a place like this?

At a Singles Bar

10. Since you don't drink, could I offer you a refreshing Long Island Iced Tea?

10. I believe that we've met before. May I ask which Sunday school you attended?

It's as simple as that! Just don't confuse them. Square² types think that Square¹ women are nerds, and Square¹ women don't even realize that Square² women exist.

But the picture will shine even brighter for a single man in the 1990s. Because, while Square¹ women seldom amount to much of anything unless they are born rich, Square² women can actually bring dazzling interpersonal skills and even great power and authority to your household, thanks to the ever-expanding role of women in the New Establishment.

It may become necessary to separate a bright, successful Square² woman from a bad choice of mate who dates other women and humiliates her in public, but this task of human refuse disposal which she could not bring herself to perform will meet her deepest need for truly square companionship as well as your own, while it flatters your own Sir Galahad fantasies.

And it's for her own good.

Marrying Up in the New Establishment

Even though you might have little to recommend you as a witty raconteur, pulse-fluttering romantic, or world-shaking success at whatever you do, be thankful that as a man you have the unfair advantage of numbers on your side. There will always be more desirable square women than there will be any semblance of desirable square men.

This enables the arguably poor excuse for a man to reach for a caliber of woman beyond his wildest teenage dreams in the days when bullies kicked sand in his face on the beach and took all the neat-looking blondes away.

For starters, you could pursue a well-heeled Square[1] woman from a fine old family. Depending on her age at the time you meet her, you can be predictably sure of what to expect from your partner.

Traditional Square[1] Female Roles

Role	Age	Behavior
Debutante	18–24	Not Knowing
Young Matron	24–35	Not Thinking
Comfortable Older Matron	35–45	Not Seeing
Dowager	45+	Not Doing

This is not to say that a Square[1] wife leads a useless life, merely an unexamined one. Square[1] types will, in fact, continue to provide the very backbone of all dog shows, many volunteer programs for the needy, important charity balls, all debutante affairs, and other machinery of life in the New Establishment Village.

Just don't expect to come home and find that your Square[1] wife has done something creative to surprise you, like flooding the guest room to make a large, exotic fish tank that you can enjoy through a glass wall of your master bedroom.

But if, in your heart, you would prefer a woman who can satisfy both your clammy adolescent fantasies *and* your responsible adult fantasies, consider the infinitely richer repertoire of choices among Square[2] women today:

New Square[2] Female Roles

Role	Age	Behavior
Student	18–22	Brilliant insights, managed relationships with men
Executive/Professional	22–35	Smart career moves, worry about relationships with men
Community Leader	35–45	Important decisions, despair about relationships with men
Guest Lecturer	45 +	Brittle insights, no relationships with men

At any age, Square[2] women of the New Establishment will be remarkably receptive to the square gentleman who shaves his stubble, listens carefully to understand her complex web of business and personal issues, manages to flash a sensitive insight every now and then, and takes care to earn her friends' approval by looking suitably grave at all times and keeping everyone on a need-to-know basis about his relationship with the Square[2]. In other words, you should always act like an Establishment elder statesman, even if you're only 23.

Best Catch, Female Under 30

7HE MOUSY SQUARE[1] DEBUTANTE

FAITH HOPE

Name: Faith Hope

Age: 23

Occupation: Charity Volunteer

Education: Isolated finishing school in Switzerland

Latest Accomplishment: Getting through coming-out party at 18

Last Book Read: *State of Massachusetts Drivers License Manual*

Haunts: Home, church, friends' homes, friends' churches, riding stables, dog kennels.

Man of Her Fantasies: Dark, brooding Adam Cartwright on "Bonanza"

Man Actually Sought: Little Joe

Men Actually Found to Date: Cads

Best Catch, Female Over 30

THE SQUARE² BUSINESSWOMAN READY TO SETTLE DOWN

Name: Ann Getty Hart

Age: 37

Occupation: President, International Women's Bank

Education: Wharton Business School, Yale Law School

Latest Accomplishment: Secured loan to keep Italy from being purchased by Libya

Last Book Read: *I'll Take Manhattan*

Haunts: 1600 Pennsylvania Avenue
10 Downing Street

Man of Her Fantasies: Prince of Liechtenstein

Man Actually Sought: You

Men Actually Found to Date: Jerks

But Beware the Pseudo-Square of Either Sex!

Ever since Huey Lewis and the News made it hip to be square, the Square population has been infiltrated by hip types who affect the outer trappings of squaredom but still harbor dangerously hip attitudes and wish only to infest others with them.

While it would be nice if God turned them all into pillars of salt so you could easily identify them, you can't count on such easy detection and should beware these warning signs.

The Pseudo-Square Single Female:

■ Wants to watch "The Tracey Ullman Show" instead of "Murder, She Wrote."

■ Pats her male partner's buttocks in public.

■ Sleeps through Sunday morning chores.

■ Wakes up wanting "brunch."

■ Looks like Cyndi Lauper wearing clothes from Ann Taylor.

The Pseudo-Square Single Male:

■ Wears bikini briefs instead of boxer shorts.

■ Thinks *It's a Wonderful Life* is corny.

■ Doesn't like it when your collie jumps up to lick his face.

■ Waits patiently for you to pick up the check.

■ Looks like Dennis Miller of "Saturday Night Live" with a recent haircut.

THE FIRST-DATE DECISION TREE
How To Arrive at the Answer to the Ultimate Decision

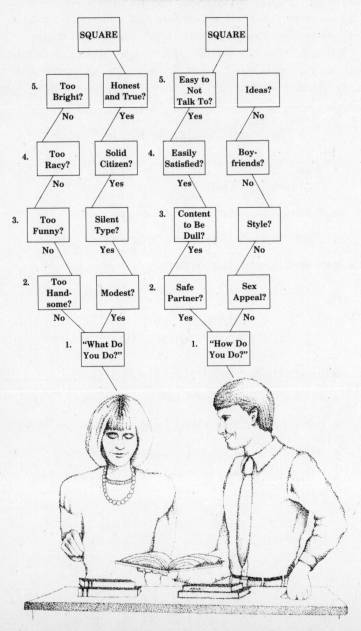

The Perfect Date
A 1992 New Year's Celibation!

Promptly at 7:30 P.M., Square Bachelor Arthur picks up Square Bachlorette Ann at her home.

Arthur dresses conservatively in a black dinner jacket, a Scottish plaid cummerbund as a rakish touch, and a little dab of Brylcreem. He greets Ann with a circumspect kiss on the cheek, smiling with fond approval at her choice of a black sackcloth and single strand of pearls. Ann squeals delightedly as Arthur pins a corsage of hardy winter greens flown in from northern Wisconsin on her bodice, poking his finger only once with the pin.

Arthur helps Ann on with her sensible mink-lined cloth coat, and escorts her to his 1958 Thunderbird convertible.

They laugh gaily in the car, through chattering teeth since Arthur has left the top down in a romantic expression of the evening's *joie de vivre,* about the fun awaiting them at the country club.

And how the club's decorating committee has outdone itself this year! With a theme of "New Years at the Andersons'," featuring a knotty pine decor, colorful balloons, and stand-up cutouts of Jim and Margaret offering canapés!

Mixing easily with the other guests, friends since kindergarten, Arthur and Ann chat amiably of steady economic growth in the year ahead, and what a good job the Rotarians are doing raising money for a new children's hospital.

The familiar strains of Guy Lombardo and his Royal Canadians excite the guests to spirited new twists on the traditional box step. Confident dancers Charlie and Jane delight one and all with an authentic Waltz of the Laplanders; then Charlie spills the martini he carries while executing a dramatic dip, and Jane barely misses the floor amidst whoops of laughter.

A serious moment restrains the revelers at 11:55 when Brigadier General Barney Stackhouse raises a glass to the American Servicemen and Women on active peacekeeping duty in the Panama Canal Zone, and Reverend Mr. Lypsinch delivers a prayer for peace in Mexico, Costa Rica, Honduras, El Salvador, and the Falklands this New Year. Then the house comes alive with anticipation as the countdown begins . . . 10! . . . 9! . . . 8! . . .

Arthur seizes this moment to tell Ann, finally, that he loves her and pops the question, "Shall we?" Inflamed with desire, they hastily insert "Prudent Passion" brand plastic tongue sleeves for a safe kiss to usher in the New Year.

Now it's midnight!

Arthur, Ann, and five other couples at their table join hands and sway back and forth in a tearful yet joyous rendition of Auld Lang Syne. Arthur casts a dubious glance at Bob Bissell, obviously a bit tight, who has evidently given Ann a huge hickey on the neck unbeknownst to either of them, and has just passed out in her lap. Thank goodness, they all agree, Bob can count on teetotaling Dan and Ginger Pinchkin, the table's designated drivers.

By 1:30 A.M. Arthur drives the T-Bird slowly and surely toward home, with Bob Bissell and Dan and Ginger Pinchkin shrieking drunk in the back seat, tickling one another and acting darn silly!

Ann pats Arthur's hand with a sweet reassuring smile that lights up her plain but radiant face. A smile that tells Arthur his good deed will not go unrewarded when they arrive at her home.

Unobserved, Arthur feels quickly in his left pants pocket to make sure there is at least one more "Prudent Passion" tongue guard left in the pack.

Betrothal for Fun and Profit

Engaged! What a wonderful way to start a relationship! Not that you would want to make lifetime plans in any heated rush, but one can't be too picky these days either. When the good-hearted young gentleman from a good family meets a good-hearted young lady from a good family, it's just . . . good sense to begin planning for a long life of contentment together. Of course, this planning process will occur a bit less haphazardly than in the seventies and eighties. And that's good, too.

Parental Arrangement

In the nineties parents who care about their children's future safety and happiness will look out for their welfare as in earlier times, with every effort to promise their own children to the off-spring of trusted friends before the prospective partners can go off and get into serious trouble on their own. Say, by fourteen or fifteen.

This should not be construed as an opportunity for greed, and attempts by the lowborn to offer their six-year-olds as choice prizes for the banker's young sons or daughters will be frowned upon.

The etiquette of parental arrangement should be observed as follows:

FATHER #1: Did you bring Jeannie's medical history?

FATHER #2: Yes. One bout of chicken pox and the whooping cough. What about you?

FATHER #1: Sure. One ear infection and a sprained ankle from football plus your basic winter flu.

FATHER #2: Hmmm. Where will you keep her then, until they get engaged in '95?

FATHER #1: Well, I've got a cousin who has a farm in Iowa.

FATHER #2: Agreed. And I'll have my son at military school.

FATHER #1: Done.

FATHER #2: Let's have a drink, then.

FATHER #1: Oh. You and Katherine drink?

Absent total parental control, the young man and woman left to their own devices should understand the code of ethics and behavior underlying all romance in the nineties.

New Rules of Engagement

1. Prior to becoming engaged, both partners must agree to deny all desire until after the marital vows have been spoken.

2. Either party may consult an engagement attorney (formerly known as "divorce" or "family" lawyers).

3. The Engagement may not be broken without written consent of the other party.

4. No written consent shall be given unless evidence of infidelity (formerly adultery) or insanity exists.

5. The young man must ask the young lady's responsible party for her hand in marriage.

Asking for permission to marry has fallen into such disuse over the past decade that the young man may need instruction in the language appropriate to different situations.

Asking the Old School Father:

"Sir, I fall on bended knee to request the honor of your daughter's hand in marriage."

Asking the Rabid Feminist Twice-Divorced Mother:

"Ms. Green, I know that Susan may be brighter and a more emotionally whole person than I, but since men mature so much more slowly than women, I would like to believe that I will grow to be her near-equal if we can be married now."

Asking the Trust Attorney:

"In the matter of Victoria Hartley, to whom I understand you provide advice and consent of a familial nature, may I request that you read this letter of intent which I have prepared in the hope of satisfying your personal concerns for Victoria as well as your fiduciary responsibilities. . . ."

The Square Wedding

All weddings are square.

Just don't let the men wear ruffled shirts or the bride any color but white.

What to Do After the Reception

Now comes the difficult part: addressing what to do with your new partner for the rest of your life. Thank goodness for the initial busy work of . . .

Writing the Fifty-Year Plan

A little organization never hurt anyone. It may seem like hard work to take those loose-leaf binders and fifty yellow legal pads along on your honeymoon, but this careful preplanning will pay off in the long run.

The First Five Years. These will be years of discovery, perhaps mounting horror, and certainly some disillusionment with the person who stood on such a lofty pedestal during the blissful months (or years) of your engagement.

Some advice:

1. *Learn to play bridge* so you will have something to do together that absolutely requires the presence of other people to talk to but *only for short conversations,* like "bid a club." Longer dialogue with others may prompt you to make compatibility comparisons with your loved one and thus entertain disturbing doubts.

2. *Stay at home as much as possible.* Absence seldom makes the heart grow fonder. Sometimes you can't even seem to remember your phone number to call home. At home, however, you will have the curious force of "propinquity" on your side. This is a scientific name for the phenomenon when two people of the opposite sex left alone together for long enough eventually decide to fall in love.

3. *Have a heart.* Consider your true love's own interests carefully. Engage in conversation designed to bring out topics that you know

your partner would like to discuss, but may be bashful about bringing up. Some effective opening lines:

> "I see that we're overdrawn $6238.00
> at the bank, and it's two weeks to payday."

> "Why don't you ever say you love me anymore?"

> "Your boss called and said you'd been fired three months ago."

> "I could have sworn we had three full bottles of gin yesterday and they all seem to be empty today."

> "Don't we have a dog?"

And when those overtures are no longer enough, it's time to engage in the greater purpose of marriage.

Making Perfectly Square Children:
The Joy of Marital Sex

There is now a new era in courtship for both sexes. The animal lures are no longer required; neither man nor woman needs to use them now. They must both be polite, chivalrous, and considerate to each other. So at last sexual intercourse is no longer a surprise or an outrage, but a surrender of two loving souls to each other.

—Dr. J. Rutgers, *How to Attain and Practice the Ideal Sex Life* (New York: Cadillac Publishing Company, 1940), p. 182.

Sex may not be much fun for some couples, but there's no reason why two healthy adults in the prime of their life together shouldn't explore the rare but delicious minutes of marital sex in the privacy of their own bedrooms.

With the stricter mores and laws likely to govern sexual conduct in the nineties, you may feel that your freedom for sexual expression will be curtailed. Not so! All it takes is a bit of imagination to put vigorous topspin on the one mode of sex which will probably be ruled permissible by the Supreme Court, the familiar "Missionary Position."

1. The Missionary Position

2. The Cavalry Mission Position

3. The Air Cavalry Mission Position

4. The Missionary-Held-Prisoner-by-Natives Position

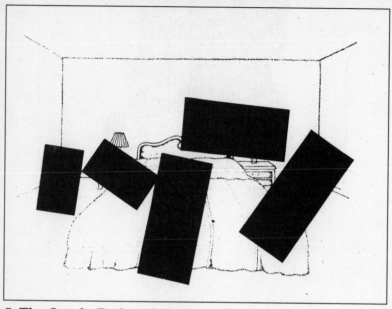

5. The Overly Zealous Missionary Position

**6. The Your-Mission-Should-You-Decide-to-
Accept-It Position**

7. The Old Spanish Mission Position

8. The Naval Mission Position

9. The Successful Mission Position

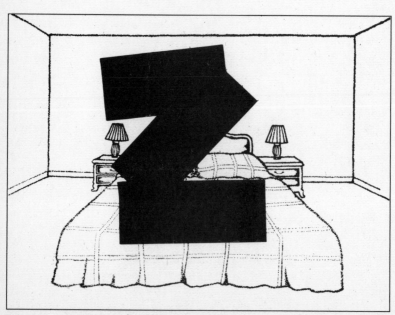

10. The Mission Impossible Position

So with a little of creativity, any couple can remain well within the laws of church and state and still "have a good one."

We Are the (Square) Children

Children, bless their little hearts, are born perfect little savages in the state of nature. Only through constant supervision, consistent discipline, and unselfish tough love can we make our children civilized enough to get along without locking a tiny playmate in the kitchen trash compactor.

This hard work required is, of course, the reason most children you see raised by parents who came of age during the sixties and seventies have not enjoyed the civilizing influence of Square parents who punish them for their own good.

Your kids are just fine, of course. Small miracles, every one. So let's look at the real behavioral problem and ask . . .

What's the Matter with Other People's Kids Today?

1. *Their Mothers Dress Them Funny.* Young children especially, who cannot complain about the silliness of their dress, are gotten up in the most bizarre of outfits patterned after the wretched excesses of their parents' wardrobes. The two-year-old child in a distressed-leather playsuit with miniature Italian hiking boots represents two hundred dollars of parental self-indulgence better invested in U.S. Savings Bonds to assure an Ivy League education when one will probably cost over $1 million per year.

   Children, little boys especially, cure this problem themselves when they reach four or five years of age and demand to begin dressing like little boys rather than being art-directed by trendy mothers.

2. *They Are Loudly Inarticulate.* Today's breed of yuppie puppies may be noisy enough, but they tend to converse as their parents do in hip jargon, a chronic chorus of "y'knows," rude phrases like "read my lips," and a punk-ValGal legacy of "awesome," "bogus," "totally," and other kidspeak which is in turn affected

by harebrained thirty-eight-year-old parents who draw scorn
from listeners of all ages.

3. *They Can't Read and Write.* Thanks to the decline of written
culture and the ascent of post-literate television programs,
most children can only read signature lines for products ad-
vertised on TV, and possibly spell WAUSAU. Written communications by the young do occur, but only with spray cans
on freeway arches at the general level of "Scool Suks."

4. *They're Rude to Adults.* Scratch a modern child of hip parents
and you will find a miniature Don Rickles. If you want to get
that close to one. A typical meeting between adult and child:
ADULT: How do you do, Scot?
CHILD: How come you got a moustache, lady?
   This much-admired "confidence" or "naturalness" comes from
giving children their space, when what they really need is close
confinement with intensive docility training.

5. *They Have No Sense of History.* Many children today pass sixth
or seventh grade with the understanding that the U.S. fought
World War II against England, due to the preponderance of
British actors selected to play German S.S. officers in movies
made for television. They are aware that the last three American Presidents were Lincoln, Kennedy, and Washington, and
recognize that the American Civil War was won in North Viet-
nam by the Spanish, due to the defeat of General Custer's
Rough Riders at San Juan Hill in 1978.

6. *They Have No Core Values.* Like their hip parents, most children today subscribe to the following principles: (1) What they
want to be when they grow up is Transformers: Robots in
Disguise. (2) Chores are places with beaches and amusement
parks, as in "The Jersey Chore." (3) J. R. Ewing is sharper
than anybody's dad, and they actively fantasize about trading
places with John Ross, Jr. (4) Any behavior is okay if RoboCop
is not looking, and (5) The most totally excellent parents a kid
could have are Madonna and Sean Penn, if they were still
together.

Raising Children in Your Own
Square Image and Likeness

Now that you have attained moral and social superiority over your hip former peers, your children will need the same careful, loving attention to how they look, sound, act, and think.

All the claptrap you've heard about "developmental stages" and "recent research in child psychology" may have led you to believe that child rearing is a complex, highly individual process. Ha! Making a perfectly square child is more akin to sound carpentry than splitting an atom, despite what the children's apologists try to tell you in those thick volumes over-referenced with Swedish studies and undernourished with plain old common sense.

Here are the only six cures for the common child you will ever need to know to square-off your offspring, by addressing each shortcoming in order:

1. *Oddly Dressed? Start Over at Brooks Brothers.* Grab your squealing infant, strip him to his diaper, and carry him under your arm to the nearest Brooks Brothers store. Introduce him to his salesperson-for-life, and choose a good, solid wardrobe from the Brooksgate selection for young men of seventeen or so. Take the garments in a bit, and you will have not only a properly dressed tyke, but a cost-effective wardrobe that the little one can grow into over many, many years. Not to mention sensible hand-me-downs for your next issue!

2. *Loud, Loutish Behavior? Practice the Old Adage, "Children Should Be Seen (Barely) and Not Heard."* If your child struggles into the room in his new oversized outfit while you are having the Vicar over for tea, and begins babbling in a way that you find at all interruptive, do not hesitate to assert your authority! Say, "Young man, you may not speak until spoken to!"

If the toddler then flies into a wild, arm-and-leg-flailing tantrum, you'll find that a wardrobe ten sizes too large has another advantage. Simply take the jacket arms and pants cuffs dangling many inches beyond hands and feet, and wrap your child up in a bundle, then carry him politely but firmly from the room and deposit him in his crib. By the time he has figured out the Houdini-like movements necessary to free himself, your guest will have long gone, with an abiding respect for your parental skills.

3. *Can't Read and Write? Use Scientific Methods.* Any responsible psychologist will tell you that positive and negative reinforcements form the backbone of learning skills. The eminent behaviorist B. F. Skinner even raised his baby daughter in a "Skinner Box," resembling a modified fish tank, to make the task of applying those tools of learning more effective.

How can you adopt the same proven approach to teaching reading and writing skills? Simply perch your child on a very high stool with the *McGuffey Reader* in front of her face and encourage her to read. Whenever she utters a word or phrase properly, permit her to climb down from the stool and rest a bit. Whenever she stumbles over the content, say in your most earnest voice, "If at first you don't succeed . . . try, try again!" Repeat it three times for emphasis.

In no time at all you will have a healthy, happy little reader chirping away, sprinting through volumes of prose and poetry like flash cards.

4. *Rude? Program Etiquette Instruction into Your Child's Computer.* Now let's turn to your child's best friend, his personal computer. Picking up a good etiquette book from the 1950s or earlier, when etiquette books were worth the paper they were printed on, borrow all relevant passages on children's behavior and program them into the nasty little know-it-all device. Heaven knows how. Use the instruction book, if it isn't printed in Japanese.

Here are two super examples from the 1956 edition of *Amy Vanderbilt's Complete Book of Etiquette* (Toronto: Doubleday).

Necessary Reminders
A boy or girl studying American history will be amused and benefited by being referred to George Washington's fifty-four maxims on personal conduct. . . . Any library can turn up frequent references to them.

Awkwardness in Children

It is important to know that increased, very notice-able awkwardness, especially at table, shown in the dropping and spilling of food, the knocking over of glasses, can be a forewarning of one of the infectious childhood diseases—scarlet fever or measles, for ex-ample—which may be followed by chorea or St. Vitus's dance. But where awkwardness seems to be part and parcel of the child, then increasing his social poise and skills may help.

Before long, your child will be curtsying like a proper little lady (daughters only, please), and using the correct fork unfail-ingly at table.

5. *Historically Shallow? Give Table Quizzes with Dinner as Reward.* It is well known that Rose Kennedy taught her sons and daughters the value of a working knowledge of current events by requiring active participation in sociopolitical discussions at dinner. With only a few million dollars judiciously spent in key precincts, that rigorous instruction catapulted the Kennedy sons to political prominence like corks rising through water.

Since you may not have the wherewithal to buy your son or daughter tickets to top national posts, you will need to put teeth into your demands for quick, sure answers to your historical questions at dinner. For instance:

LITTLE JOHN: Mommy, I don't have any food on my plate.

MOTHER: Naturally, dear. Now, who fought in the Hundred Years' War?

LITTLE JOHN: Mommy, I'm hungry!

FATHER: Let's not be too tough on the child, dear. Okay, son, for this tablespoon of corn . . . who was Franklin Delano Roosevelt's Vice President?

LITTLE JOHN: (Gulp) Uh, Truman?

FATHER: Well done! Now, for this fish stick, who bought Sherman Adams his vicuna coat?

6. *No Core Values? Plug in the Toddler-Safe Square Values System.* The readymade values system in Chapter Four is so simple even a hip adult could assemble and use it in thirty minutes. Think how much easier it will be for your child!

And the Square Value System (SVS) is "baby proofed" to be safe for children of any age.

See? You can have square children too, in the wink of an eye.

Should you have any doubts that you're doing the right thing for your children, consider the advice given by square syndicated pediatrician John Rosemond:

> . . . *Today's children are not being sufficiently frustrated. . . . In 1986 a group of researchers found that four years after high school graduation, almost half of all young adults continue to live with their parents. This is double the number of "nesters" in 1976. When asked to explain this alarming trend, the researchers basically said that this generation of children was given almost everything they wanted. As a result, they have difficulty successfully adapting to the requirements of emancipation.*
>
> *If you aren't doing so already, you can begin seeing to your obligation by giving your children regular, daily doses of "Vitamin No." This inexpensive verbal balm is one of the most character-building two-letter words in the English language. It is surely as essential to a child's growth and development as vitamins A, B, and C.*
>
> *If you say it, and your child falls on the floor and screams, consider it a job well done.*
>
> —"Children Need to Be Frustrated," *Miami Herald,* November 15, 1987, p. 3G.

Now that you've learned about love in the nineties, our work here is almost done. We can finally turn to the perks and privileges of the good life as you'll live it in the New Establishment.

HOW TO SAVE $288,900 WITH EVERY SQUARE CHILD YOU MAKE

Yuppy Puppy
From 1 mo. to 21 yrs.

Square Child
From 1 mo. to 21 yrs.

Yuppy Puppy		Square Child	
1. Clothing by Baby Dior, Kidoko, Ralph Lauren ($4,000 average cost per year)	$84,000	1. Clothing by grandparents and Brooks Brothers ($500 average cost per year)	$10,000
2. Toys by Sesame Street, Mattell, Apple, and Porsche Leasing ($6,000 average cost per year)	$30,000	2. Toys by Goodwill Industries or purchased by child (average cost per year)	$4,000
3. Child psychiatry (6–12)	$24,000	3. Child labor	$–0–
4. Summer camp in Italy (8–12)	$50,000	4. Scouting (8–12)	$2,000

5. Trendy prep school (12–17)	$60,000	5. Public school where you got the principal his pay raise	$–0–
6. Private liberal arts college for spoiled kids (18–21)	$72,000	6. West Point or full academic scholarship to Ivy League School	$–0–
TOTAL	$320,000	TOTAL	$16,200
		YOU SAVE:	$288,900

six

NEW ESTABLISHMENT 101:

Assuming the Reins of Control

■ ■ ■ ■ ■ ■

In this chapter you will learn:

- what to wear, drive, and say when duty calls.
- where to live in the nineties, and where to go safely on vacation.
- what to do at the country club besides watching the Japanese golf.
- how to putter around the house.
- sound investments for after the crash.
- how to live through your children.

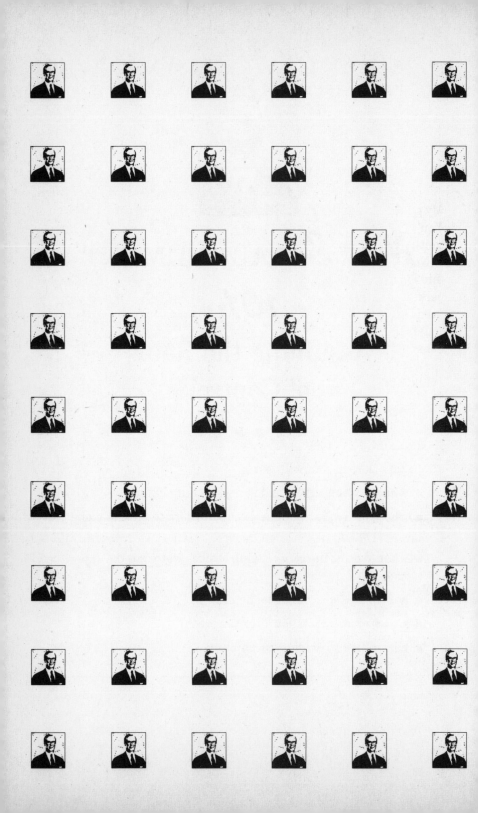

*C*ongratulations! And welcome home! My goodness, but you've come a long way in a few short chapters. You've learned your lessons well, and shown remarkable stick-to-it-iveness besides!

Now, just as promised, you stand ready to be ushered proudly into the New Establishment with full honors, eligible for all the perks and privileges that members command. Of course, you will need to know certain tiny secrets that will lend you, the recently squared individual, the same easy familiarity with New Establishment thought and behavior that those who were always perfectly square possess as their birthright.

Like how to act . . .

*W*HEN *D*UTY *C*ALLS

There's just one small matter left to settle between us: payment of your dues. Not the money kind, which will be painless, but the terribly-humiliating-and-dangerous-fraternity-initiation kind that used to be called hazing.

You see, everyone who's made it into the Establishment as an adult, practically from the dawn of time, has done so at the great personal sacrifice of performing certain tasks that nobody in the Establishment particularly wanted to be identified with.

Dwight David Eisenhower had to win World War II before the powers that be at home could, in good conscience, make him President of Columbia University. Lee Iacocca had to save the laughably lost cause of Chrysler Motors from bankruptcy and thousands of jobs before he could be entrusted with sanding and painting the Statue of Liberty for her birthday celebration. Jacqueline

Kennedy-Onassis-Kennedy needed to become First Lady, national heroine, and billionaire's surviving spouse before she could attain the coveted post of Editor at an Establishment publishing house.

Who Will Call?

The Board Member Who Wants Out. Your first invitation to join the board of directors of a company or the board of trustees of some nonprofit institution will probably come from a desperate member who feels the obligation of self-replacement before running out on a no-win situation. For instance, she might have been asked to head a fact-finding committee that will attract public attention, and she is in reality a transvestite with self-doubts about revealing five o'clock shadow on the six o'clock news. Or the board member of a public company may be looking to retire in some country without a U.S. extradition treaty on the eve of a full-dress audit.

So always count on rough sailing ahead. If it's a corporate board, you will be the one asked to inform the newly hired president that the board now wants his resignation. If made a university's trustee, you will surely be charged with finding some contractual reason to fire a ninety-six-year-old professor with tenure who weeps piteously in all his classes. And whatever the board wants, you must accomplish. So long as it's morally defensible, of course.

The Desperate Fund-Raiser with Nowhere Else to Turn. Often a charitable organization or Political Action Committee (PAC) falls so out of favor with the tenor of the times that its fund-raisers can't seem to turn up a subway token. For instance, the Friends of Chain Smokers PAC, not funded by the tobacco industry, may be short of its annual goal of raising $1 million for the legal defense of preschool teachers who refuse to give up their right to smoke in the classroom.

If you have earned the reputation of a take-charge-and-make-it-happen type, you'll probably be asked to breathe new life into a dying cause. Then you will be forced to sit across the desk from powerful men and women and ask them to donate money for activities they may view as dimly as cannibalism. They might also, however, admire your energy and perseverance thrown so vigorously over the cliff of the wrong cause, and enlist you to help them in some obscure pet project of their own, like getting a rival developer's building placed on the Historical Preservation list so he'll have to take out all the air conditioners.

The Lonely Club Member. You may one day be solicited by the member of a prized club who is so boring or loathsome to others that nobody wants to keep him, or her, company. This will be your duty and, because the other members perceive a strong need for finding the self-orphaned member a playmate, nobody will be likely to blackball your application.

This will slip you under the front door, where you may discreetly make other contacts as you faithfully execute your job of amusing your ticket of admission. For instance:

YOUR MENTOR: Let us have another round of drinks, and I will tell you about the year I turned five.

YOU: Sounds tempting, but perhaps we could play a rubber of bridge in the game room instead.

YOUR MENTOR: No, I tried bridge once and didn't like it.

YOU: Backgammon?

YOUR MENTOR: No. Played that once and disliked it as well.

YOU: Squash?

YOUR MENTOR: Sorry, did it once with no great fondness.

YOU: Badminton, then?

YOUR MENTOR: No. Played it only once with my son.

YOU: Your only child, I presume?

The Boss's Office with a Problem Requiring a Human Flak Jacket. For many, the Establishment comes calling when every-

184 • Dare to Be Square

one already in it at your firm has tried to attack some unsolvable business problem and failed. Then, with little to lose and fear setting in, your chief executive may reach down into the bowels of the corporation where you work to find additional people to hurl at the problem, in the blind hope that one will stick and succeed.

For example, your company may have a key customer for its manufactured product, who happens to be a bullying, unprincipled moron. This customer has made a gross error through inattention to his own job, which your firm must now cover up by manufacturing a million toggle switches or whatever it is that you make by the following day or the customer will go elsewhere. But your facilities can produce only 100,000 toggle switches a day, and nobody has the nerve to explain this to the sweaty, scowling customer.

Now, if you are the one with the quick fix, which may be simply to inject the customer with a sleeping drug in your office and wake him up ten days later when his order is ready, you will undoubtedly be moved immediately to the office adjoining your president's, and elevated to the position of solving all his or her business and personal problems.

What to Wear

Clothes don't make the man or woman, but the wrong apparel can certainly brand you as "unfit for duty" when the call arrives.

Some may suggest to you that looking properly square can be accomplished merely by wearing clothes and a hairstyle twenty or thirty years out of date and choosing particularly unflattering eyeglasses that were never in style anywhere. Not so. These are the same people who will show up at an Admiral's reception on board a U.S. battleship dressed in a Captain's cap and "Anchors Aweigh" T-shirt! Dressing to pass New Establishment muster remains a subtle and serious business, reflecting a proper "attitude" of dress as well as the correct choice of fabrics and fitting.

Acceptable	*Unacceptable*
1. Fabrics from sheep.	1. Fabrics from cattle or chemistry labs.
2. Colors that were worn to church services in the 1600s: blue, gray, black with white collars.	2. Colors that will look different on a color TV than in black and white.
3. Simple, sacklike tailoring.	3. Shape-fitting apparel, unless the shape you have chosen for yourself is a pear.
4. Functional jewelry: watches for watching, simple pearl chokers for choking, signet rings for signing documents (old families).	4. Purely decorative jewelry: nonmarital rings, watches with diamonds or depth finders, chains unattached to a vest-pocket watch, earrings larger than necessary for plugging the tiny holes in certain women's ears.
5. Traditional accessories: white handkerchiefs for colds, and an extra one for handing to people in tearful distress, cuffs on pants to collect change that falls from pockets, women's scarfs for tying up hair that would otherwise blow around seductively.	5. Trendy accessories, such as giant-sized paper clips in women's hair, men's handbags used in the seventies and eighties to carry drugs, guerrilla gunbelts and camouflage face paint for women, ostrich coats for men.

New Establishment men need patronize only one store over the entire course of their lives, which is Brooks Brothers. The styles practically never change, making the chore of shopping at any age, in whatever century, a simple matter of going into the store with a checkbook once a year and asking your trusted lifetime salesperson what you appear to need.

Proper role models for male dress include Pat Boone (for young men under thirty) and Bing Crosby (for the more mature man), as shown.

Women of the New Establishment will find shopping a bit more demanding, since three or four stores still exist from the 1800s that permit you flexibility in choosing clothing designed to keep alive traditions that were perhaps dead long before you were born.

Proper role models for female dress include the models of the 1950s, as illustrated.

■ ■ ■ ■ ■

SQUARE WEAR

■ ■ ■ ■ ■

Sophisticated in Seattle

The feeling: Black and white set the stage for a Nineties Night on the Town.

Who says neo-Puritans need to be dull?

Bing is back! And always in style! Here's a blazer with family crest, squared off for a semiformal evening at the country club.

Business in Baltimore

The feeling: Life in the nineties isn't all black and white, but shades of gray in between.

A delightful departure from the Yuppie floppy bow, this everyday suit for women of the New Establishment spells a businesslike "let's roll up our sleeves and trousers" attitude.

Casual in Cleveland

No poodles, please! Just a simple statement in white and gray that's right from soda fountain to snack bar.

**For Pat Boone, plenty of homework and clean white bucks
spell success in business and personal life.**

SQUARECUTS

The Flattop. *For young men of the nineties, the correct hairstyle is a "carpenter's dream."*

The Stovetop. *A casual, curved style always worn with black, modeled by laid-back neo-Puritan Perry Como.*

The Nunstop. *For serious-minded young women, no style at all plus singularly unflattering eyeglasses says there's more going on upstairs than a permanent wave!*

The Hilltop. *A small but perfectly scaled model of Mount Everest's peak worn just "because it's there!"*

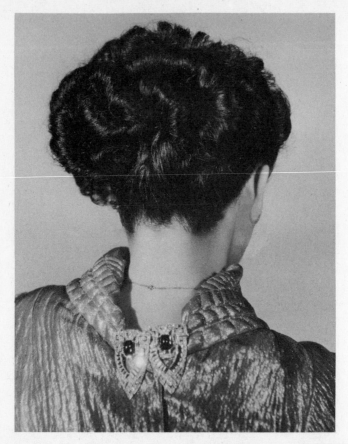

The Two-Lane Backtop. *Naturalists will note two "unconstructed" strips of neckline, shown off with a proud upsweep.*

■ ■ ■ ■ ■ ■

What to Drive

When duty calls, you do not want to screech up to the door of the Establishment in a BMW, honking loudly for an attendant. Driving foreign cars will be considered, at best, déclassé during the Restoration Era and, at worst, unpatriotic. Have you looked at the yen versus the dollar lately?

The problem, of course, is that they don't build American cars like they used to. Instead of a good, solid door slam, we have computer chips that try to regulate too many operations, thus go berserk and constantly need attention. In place of AM radio blasting out good, wholesome songs like "Hey, Paula (I want to marry you)" through one speaker in the dash, we need to worry about graphics equalizers and a dozen speakers, half of which you can't even see, that all develop hissing noises when the thirty-day warranty expires.

The solution: back to the future. In the Restoration Era cars that were designed and built to both accommodate and delight square adults will return in full-sized glory. Best square car maker: Ford, going all the way back to founder Henry Ford's sound philosophy, "Give 'em any color they want so long as it's black." Best Ford of all: the "Square Bird" (1958–1960 Thunderbird).

In case you're unsure of which fifties car to choose for the nineties, here's the lowdown you won't find in *Consumer Reports:*

Instead of Buying a Hip:	You Can Move Up to a Square:	And Save This Much to Give to the United Way:
1. 1988 Mercedes 500 SEL Coupe	1956 Lincoln Continental Mark II Coupe	$40,000
2. 1988 Volvo Station Wagon	1956 Ford Country Squire	$17,000
3. 1988 Saab Turbo Convertible	1958 Ford Thunderbird Hardtop or Convertible	$25,000–$30,000
4. 1988 BMW 325I 4-door Sedan	1960 Ford Falcon 4-door Sedan	$23,000

■ ■ ■ ■ ■ ■

SQUARE WHEELS

The Ford Family of Fine Cars for the Restoration Era

■ ■ ■ ■ ■ ■

Square with "Continental" Flair. *1956 Lincoln Continental Mark II. The successful professional of the nineties used to Mercedes and BMW Eurostyling will feel at home in this sculpted beauty good enough to be named after an American President.*

Square with Children. *1956 Ford Town and Country Wagon, the woodie that's both an oldie and a goodie, will seat Mom, Dad, and three perfectly square children comfortably with room for a whole litter of cocker spaniels in back.*

Square 'n' Style-Free. *1960–61 Ford Falcon.* **For those who value frugality over fashion (and who won't?). America's very first compact car makes a welcome comeback.**

Square 'n' Sporty. *1958–60 Thunderbird.* **Known to aficio-
nados as the "Square Bird," this star of "Perry Mason" reruns promises to become the Restoration Era cult mobile.**

... And a Square Splash! *1959 Amphicar. Just when you thought it was safe to drive your car into the water, the Amphicar reappears! A snappy convertible on the road, the clever amphibian will do a sedate five knots on the water. Honk once if you come by land, two if by sea.*

DOING *YOUR* DUTY FOR *HOME* AND COUNTRY

Once you're all prepared with the right clothes and car, of course, you will have to actually do your duty. But this is the simple part.

Saying "No" to Family. Let's begin at home, with your own spouse and children. It will be your duty as a responsible adult to say "no" clearly and firmly to all of the wrong influences. You must practice letting out a hearty, resounding "no" to amusement parks and video arcades (too unwholesome), designer sheets (too vain), artificial logs in the fireplace (too easy), most television (too frivolous), Yuppie Puppie friends (too obnoxious), Ben & Jerry's Brownie Bars (too tempting), unsupervised dating (too risky), coming-of-age movies (too sexy), adventure movies (too violent), the great majority of newspapers and magazines (too hip), and sunglasses (too cool).

Saying "No" for Your Community's Own Good. Often disreputable, unwholesome elements in your very own home town will put forth plans for a Church of Satan or other unwanted edifice before your zoning board.

This will be your opportunity to stand up before your neighbors and say "no" to Miami Vice–style buildings, hip boutiques and haircutters, malls where teenagers congregate unchaperoned (in the Restoration Era, it will be critical to provide no place *but* home for teenagers), commercial schools that teach young people how to be blackjack dealers, foreign film festivals, foreign car dealerships, foreign food franchises, foreign-sounding investors, housing developments with foreign names like "Les Maisons de Greed," and foreign churches like the Soviet Orthodox Church of the Wrong Assumption.

Saying "No" for Your Country. It will *not* be permissible in the Restoration Era to sell military secrets to foreign powers, even though it may have been the growth industry of the 1980s.

Be vigilant to go on "verbal alert" if you ever hear telltale icebreakers like:

BALD WEASEL-NOSED MAN IN OVERSIZED LEATHER COAT:	My, that looks like a heavy briefcase! Let me help you with it, if you could just hold this fat packet of hundred-dollar bills for me.
DARK, SLAVIC WOMAN WITH BLOND WIG:	Say, big boy, I vunder if I could trade you my lacy underwear for those laser diagrams at my *dacha* . . . er . . . little house.

Remember, loose hips as well as loose lips sink ships!

Where to Give, Where to Sit: Square PACs and Boards

While you must be generous with your time and money in supporting worthy causes, take care to avoid those unworthy of your attention.

This becomes a thorny problem today because you can't always tell from the name of an organization exactly what cause you will be supporting. For example, you might want to join the altruistic souls who formed the "Good Samaritan Coalition" in Washington to help those who have fallen by the wayside and need assistance, until you find out that it is actually a political action group of the Hazardous Materials Advisory Council, working on legislation to protect chemical and petroleum companies that assist in hazardous-materials emergencies from unwanted lawsuits.

There are just a few of the suitably square political action committees (PACs) and organizations that should be viewed with favor when you are asked to make a donation or sit on the board.[1]

BANKPAC of the American Bankers Association labors to help elect representatives to the U.S. Congress who have demonstrated a fond concern for the banking industry and wish to see America's banks prosper and grow. Phone: (202) 663–5114.

[1] Encyclopedia of Associations, 22nd edition (Detroit, Mich.: Gale Publishing, 1987).

MESSIES ANONYMOUS, conducts workshops to help chonically disorganized people (Messies) learn proper housekeeping techniques. Phone: (305) 271–8404.

WAMOC, the Women's Auxiliary to the Military Order of the Cootie, is composed of women doing volunteer work in hospitals, rest homes, and mental institutions. Phone: (419) 298–2681.

Warning!! Yuppie PAC!! The ACPA, or American Citizens for Political Action, announces its mission as furthering the interests of "Young, upwardly mobile professionals."

Other groups doing good works include the Big Band Enthusiasts for Peace Through Strength, the Garden Clubs of America, the National Pest Control Association, and the National Association of Manufacturers.

Where to Work: The Squarest Companies

It just stands to reason that you will be hand-picked for the New Establishment sooner if you work for a fine old firm like Morgan Guaranty Bank than if you breeze into a hip boutique and punch a SWATCH time clock every day.

Here are nine firms that make better sense for doing business fair and square, chosen for a corporate culture that rewards the responsible, a quality product, and community service.[2]

---

[2]Adapted in part from Ross and Kathryn Petras, *Inside Track* (New York, Random House, 1986), and Robert Levering, Milton Moscowitz, and Michael Katz, *The 100 Best Companies to Work For in America* (Reading, Mass.: Addison-Wesley, 1985).

Firm	Culture
1. Morgan Guaranty Trust Banking Headquarters: New York, NY	Makes money the old-fashioned way. A dark-mahogany Establishment financial institution.
2. Hallmark Cards Greeting Cards Headquarters: Kansas City, MO	Model of the happy corporate family, with no layoffs, cynics, or ostentatious cars in the employee garage.
3. Johnson & Johnson Consumer Products Headquarters: New Brunswick, NJ	The company that makes Band-Aids lives by a credo that places babies and mothers ahead of stockholders.
4. Deere & Company Farm Equipment Headquarters: Moline, IL	Well-loved by America's farmers for excellent products and employees for the squeaky-clean factory called "The Versailles of the Cornfields."
5. J. C. Penney Retailing Headquarters: New York, NY	The chain most obviously founded by a minister's son. Employees are known as "associates," then "partners." Community good works are legendary. Least likely to be accused of a hip or trendy fashion attitude.
6. Knight-Ridder Newspapers, TV Stations, Information Services Headquarters: Miami, FL	Believes in traditional American values. It was a Knight-Ridder newspaper that exposed philanderer Gary Hart in 1987. The last annual report used Norman Rockwell–style illustrations throughout.

Firm	Culture
7. Reader's Digest Association Magazines and Books Headquarters: Pleasantville, NY	A pleasant place to work on uplifting articles. The Georgian colonial building comes with a community garden and plots for individual employees to tend.
8. IBM Business Equipment Headquarters: Armonk, NY	Practically a religion. Managers are judged on how they treat employees. Customers are supposed to be satisfied. There's a country club for all IBM people with an 18-hole golf course.
9. The U.S. Attorney's Office America's Law Firm Headquarters: Washington, DC	The avenging prosecutorial ethic still guides the office. Hard work, low pay, and the constant temptation to sell your soul to a private firm for more money.

Be There and Be Square:
Sensible Cities

If you don't feel that your current home offers the wholesome surroundings for a real life rather than just a lifestyle, you can always do what President Reagan said while people were still listening. Vote with your feet.

Here are ten cities in the United States (and one in Canada, which is on the average 20 percent squarer than the United States) to meet your need for a safe place to be yourself.

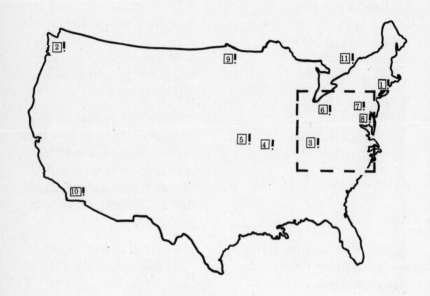

1. Hartford, Connecticut

2. Seattle, Washington

3. Louisville, Kentucky

4. St. Louis, Missouri

5. Kansas City, Missouri

6. Cleveland, Ohio

7. Philadelphia, Pennsylvania

8. Baltimore, Maryland

9. St. Paul, Minnesota

10. San Diego, California

11. Ottawa, Canada

City of the Future I. St. *Louis will boast the nation's largest McDonald's, shown here under construction for a September 1, 1995, Opening Day.*

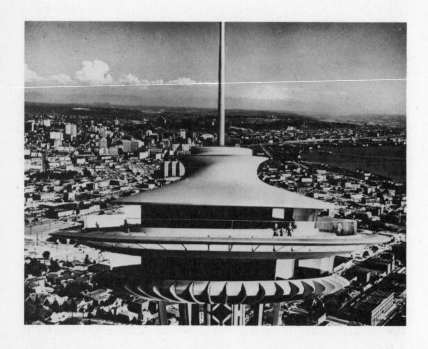

City of the Future II. *The J. Copacino family of Seattle stands aboard the floating bridge of the first supersonic cruise ship, S.S. Queen Anne, planned to launch in 1993. Seattle's Boeing created this majestic lady for smooth sailing at any altitude.*

7HE GOOD STUFF: ESTABLISHMENT PERKS AND PRIVILEGES

Let's relax a bit, kick off those heavy brogues, and make yourself a stiff martini. Heck, you deserve it. You've changed jobs. Moved to a saner city. Gotten a little messy doing volunteer work at the animal hospital. Traded that new BMW convertible you used to like so much for a 1960 Thunderbird. Everybody's proud of you! Really!

See how much better you feel having sacrificed and sweated your way into the Establishment, pulling yourself up by the boot-straps every inch of the way? Now you're ready to enjoy life full-measure because you've *earned* it.

Gee whiz. Kind of makes you want to have another martini, but hold off while we have one last chat . . . and a *fun* chat this time . . . about your wonderful new life as a Responsible Adult.

The Country Club

If you haven't joined a country club yet, it's time. The purpose of a country club is, simply stated, to have a place where (1) you don't have to blow an artery to get a table from some insufferable Frenchman, (2) there will be only a few people who don't look, act, and think the way you do, and most of them work in the kitchen. To make sure you're getting part two right, you should be extremely picky about which club you join.

Not Too Racy, Please! The last surprise you want is to show up at your club and be brushed aside at the door by a crowd of European glitterati or, worse, loud-mouthed developers.

Look for telltale signs of weeping hipness or too-democratic behavior. White dinner jackets worn by members signal trouble. So do big purple Lincolns with windows cut out in heart shapes.

One highly positive sign is when members play the sport of curling.

212 • *Dare to Be Square*

■ ■ ■ ■ ■ ■

CURLING SWEEPS SQUARE AMERICA!
Curling has been called Scotland's own game, and it is played there with a passion. However, it is one of Canada's most popular participant sports and is gaining popularity in the northern United States.

SHUFFLEBOARD ON ICE!
Curling is played on a smooth ice surface, 138 by 14 feet, with a tee at each end. These tees are situated at the center of the "house," a target of concentric circles. Only stones placed within the house can score.

CURL!
The captain, or "skip," directs each team's strategy. He must be a master tactician because he directs each stone delivered by his teammates, and he must also be the best curler on the team because he curls last, when the ice is littered with stones. To start play, the skip stands at the target end of the ice, placing a broom on the ice for his rinkmate to aim at. His rinkmate, his eye on the skip's broom, tries to "curl" the stone where the skip has directed.

SWEEP!
If the skip decides the stone is going to stop short of its target, he gives the command, "Sweep," and his rinkmates do just that. Originally a janitorial duty done to clear the ice of twigs and other debris blown there by the wind, sweeping is today an entrenched part of the game. It makes the ice slicker and helps the stone slide farther than it normally would.

BRRR!
Curlers dress informally, without uniforms, and of course warmly. Some curlers have been known to play outdoors in temperatures of thirty degrees below zero.[3]

■ ■ ■ ■ ■ ■

[3]*The Sports Encyclopedia,* edited by Ford Harris (New York: Praeger, 1976).

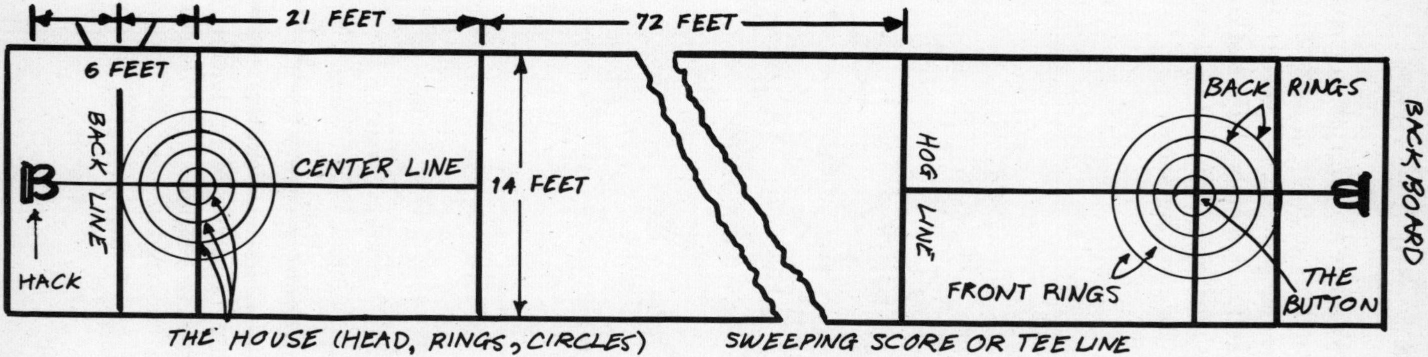

THE CURLING FIELD

Labels on the diagram:

BACK BOARD

BACK RINGS

THE BUTTON

FRONT RINGS

HOG LINE

SWEEPING SCORE OR TEE LINE

72 FEET

14 FEET

21 FEET

6 FEET

CENTER LINE

THE HOUSE (HEAD, RINGS, CIRCLES)

BACK LINE

HACK

Best Club Amusements. The most fun one can have on an American golf course is watching a group of Japanese visitors play. Because the game is so dearly loved in Japan but there is so little land available for it, golf club memberships cost companies over $1 million and players must race through 18 holes at a breakneck pace to make way for the next foursome.

The second best time is drinking martinis or bourbon on the rocks, playing whist and canasta with friends, then sitting on the club steps swaying back and forth waiting to be driven home.

Best Waiting Activity: Counting Cadillacs, the endangered autospecies, in the club parking lot. More than ten suggests that you are either in Detroit or Florida.

Getting to Stay Home

The best part of being a responsible adult, truth be told, is not having to go out at all if you don't feel like it. No more cursing at cuff links that won't fit through the little holes because you really don't want to get dressed up in that starchy shirt and those itchy pants at all. You just want to stay home and curl up with a good book, or into a fetal position.

Not Too Racy, Please. You needn't pretend to like those ice-cold glass bricks and sharp-edged chairs inspired by the Marquis de Sade anymore. Move out of that condo tiled by your decorator in jagged rock, so you cut your feet every time you step out of the shower, and find a nice colonial-style house furnished in the comfortable nondescript mode. You'll know it when you see it. You'll feel at home.

So long, Frank Lloyd Wright.

A real home for the nineties.

Best Home Amusements. The very best time to be had at home is called "puttering around the house," which means wandering about doing this and that of a constructive nature, including but not limited to gardening, fixing things that are broken, building interesting projects, playing lawn games such as badminton and croquet in the summer, and winding up the day having a drink with friends and neighbors, with the school principal or minister dropping by to thank you for whatever good works you've done lately.

You may need special instruction on "puttering around the house," because it hasn't exactly been the hot topic on the Letterman show. To start with, there are two simple flowers anyone can grow which are square in nature. One is the daisy, which you sow in late summer, then transplant with mulch for the winter. The other is the sunflower, a big daisy that you sow in fertile, well-drained soil. You can then harvest the seeds and use them in a bird feeder.[4]

[4]Conrad B. Link and Francis C. Stark, *The Whole Seed Catalog* (New York: Grosset & Dunlap, 1976), p. 73.

As soon as you finish sowing the seeds, you should continue puttering by immediately starting your bird feeder. If you live in the country, you may wish to build a revolving birdhouse on your weathervane which, on a windy day, will keep your rooftop a "seedbed" of activity much like a busy aircraft carrier, with birds diving down toward the door, aborting their landing just as the wind shifts, and circling for another approach while still other birds attempt to lift off from the crazily spinning birdhouse. If you live in an urban area, you will probably want to attract the most common bird in your neck of the woods by building an authentic American log cabin for pigeons, or the more elaborate Swiss Pigeon Chalet.[5]

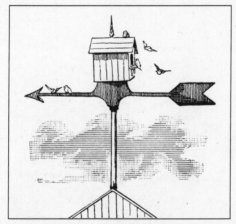

Robin roulette: a fast-revolving birdhouse.

[5]*The Compleat Craftsman,* compiled by Martin Lawrence (New York: Main Street Press, 1977), pp. 12–18.

An urban log cabin for pigeons.

A swiss pigeon chalet.

Square Trivia: The Bible Game. Here's a game the whole family can enjoy that's semireligious and fully educational. All you need is several players, a Bible, and a few pads of paper. The object is to know your Bible, cold, or to be so clever at inventing passages that *might* have come from the Bible, you could fool the Parson himself!

The first player begins by taking the Bible, turning at random to any verse, and naming the verse aloud like "Psalms 2:23," but stopping short of reading the verse itself. Then he or she writes the *actual* verse on a piece of paper, while all the other players write what *they* think the verse says. The first player then collects each player's "verse," shuffles them all, and reads them aloud with the correct one buried in the group. The other players guess which verse is real.

The best Bible Game player ever would have been Ida Stover, President Eisenhower's mother (if she ever chose to play), since she reportedly memorized more than 3000 verses of the Bible!

Barbecuing Thick Steaks. Don't you miss those five-inch-thick beauties sizzling juicily on the grill, seared with a squirt of lemon and once over lightly with the pepper mill? What the hey, why not throw a couple on, with bourbon on the rocks all around! And pass the salt, please! Just put the stuffed zucchini back in the fridge for the next trendies who stop by, maybe in 1998.

SQUARE MEALS

The Puritan Tradition

Millard Fillmore, President of the United States from 1850 to 1853, distinguished his administration with study, hard work, and temperance, eschewing frivolity and luxury. Still, he regarded entertaining as a solemn, unsmiling duty and thus kept Puritanism alive in the White House mess.

Here are his authentic recipes so you can too.[6]

SHAKER FLANK STEAK

Meat, potatoes, and vegetables were the ingredients of life for the Fillmores. Fixed appetizingly in this fashion, they are delicious fare for all of us.

Flank Steak	Onions
Flour	Carrot
Butter or margarine	Celery
Salt and pepper	Lemon juice
Potatoes, diced	Ketchup

Score both sides of a 2-pound flank steak diagonally. Dust with 1 tablespoon flour. Brown the steak in a skillet in 1½ tablespoons butter or margarine. Sprinkle with ¾ teaspoon salt and ¼ teaspoon pepper. Add 2 large peeled raw potatoes diced in fairly large cubes. Add 2 small onions, chopped, and 1 carrot chopped in medium chunks, as well as 1 stalk chopped celery. Pour over all the juice of ½ lemon and ⅓ cup ketchup. Cover skillet and simmer slowly for an hour or longer, until steak is tender. Serve with the vegetable sauce over the steak. Serves 4.

[6]Poppy Cannon and Patricia Brooks, *The Presidents' Cookbook* (New York: Bonanza Books, 1968), pp. 202–204.

RESURRECTION PIE

How fitting a title for this dish of the straitlaced Millard Fillmores! The recipe came originally from the North Country of England, home of Fillmore's family. It resembles the hot pots of Lancashire, which called for equal parts of liver, steak, and rabbit. Made by the English settlers in New York State, beef or pork liver and cuts similar to round steak were used instead. This "pie" has no crust, but pie it was called in Fillmore's day, so pie it shall be.

Liver	Bacon
Round steak	Salt and pepper
Onions	Water or consommé
Potatoes	

Cut the meat—1 pound beef or pork liver and 1 pound round steak—into slices ½ inch thick. Slice 2 onions and 6 medium potatoes ¼ inch thick. Arrange in layers in a well-greased casserole, beginning with a layer of meat sprinkled with 3 slices of lean bacon cut into bits, then a layer of onions and potatoes mixed, then meat and bacon again. Season with ½ teaspoon salt and ¼ teaspoon pepper. Cover with cold water or consommé. Make a topping of onions and potatoes. Dot with butter. Cover tightly with a lid or aluminum foil and bake 1½ hours in a moderate (350° F.) oven. *Modern adaptation:* Remove the lid and allow the dish to brown delicately for the last 15 minutes of cooking. Serve sprinkled with chopped parsley. A good accompaniment is a dish of sliced tomatoes and leaf spinach, served with a tart vinegar dressing. Serves 6.

Dinner in a Jiffy!
You can prepare family treats in forty-five minutes, without a microwave oven, with skip-a-step mixes and preparation pared to bare essentials:[7]

BOLOGNA BAKE

¾ pound big bologna, diced (2 cups)

1 cup celery slices

¼ cup sliced stuffed olives

4 hard-cooked eggs, diced

¼ cup chopped onion

1 tablespoon prepared mustard

Dash pepper

¾ cup mayonnaise

1 cup crushed potato chips

Combine all ingredients except potato chips. Place in 8¼ × 1¾-inch round ovenware cake dish; sprinkle with crushed potato chips. Bake in hot oven (400° F.) 20 to 25 minutes. Makes 4 or 5 servings.

▪ ▪ ▪ ▪ ▪

[7]*Meals in Minutes*, edited by *Better Homes and Gardens* (New York: Meredith, 1963), pp. 7–9.

Required Reading

When you're ready to take your news and views without cute, colorful chatter about celebrities, trendy analysis and the "human" side of the story, you will sure as fate reach for two sources of thoroughly responsible thought:

U.S. News & World Report, the adult news magazine. Here you will shudder before an unvarnished wrap-up of the world as it really is. Cold and hard.

Articles from the last cheery New Year's edition include:

- "The Burden-Sharing Blues; It's Time for Nations to Behave Like Adults."

- "Yugoslavia: Where Balkanizing Gets Its Name and Still Deserves It."

- "Bootstrap Time in a Luckless Land: American Samaritans Confront the Ethiopian Famine."

A "News You Can Use" section tells you how to avoid throwing your money away in the latest investment you've been reading about in all the other magazines.

The Wilson Quarterly, the adult journal. Because world events can seem like "Nightmare on Elm Street: Freddy Becomes President" after a few months of taking *U.S. News & World Report* straight, you may wish to calm yourself with a leisurely evening of perusing this *Quarterly* published by the Wilson Center, a diverse group of scholars who lay crises out in longhand. Somehow nothing looks so bad when it's explored at Wilsonian length. Some subject areas from recent issues:

- "The Maritime World" (from the lost Atlantis through an analysis of Soviet shipbuilding).

- "Astronomy to Astrophysics."

- "The Dutch."

Books and other periodicals are reviewed in such a way that you will never have to read them if you can't find the time.

TV with Redeeming Value

Who says television today is a vast wasteland of unspeakable violence and venal role models for children, sycophantic talk show hosts, mindlessly inadequate news, celebrities with overblown egos, obnoxious commercials, fraudulent psychological counseling, petulant soap operas, moronic situation comedies, and legalized pornography? You didn't see it here.

With a little selectivity, today's new Couch Potatoes and little Tater Tots can easily find wholesome entertainment merely by sticking to comfortable reruns of shows from the 1950s, and even a few worthy programs produced within the past twenty years.

The key is to provide proper role models for your children and your spouse. Today young viewers who have no Square Value System plugged in at an early age learn their ethical standards from television. A *New York Times* study found that high school students form their sense of right and wrong from TV villains![8]

Alexis of "Dynasty": "[She's] bad. Like she's vicious and bold and glamorous. And she's everything that any woman would want to be."

J. R. Ewing of "Dallas": "I sort of admire the way he can just corrupt everybody and not even let it affect him."

Here are some new, improved role models for strictly supervised viewing:

The Square "L.A. Law": "Perry Mason" Reruns. Not the new Perry Mason movies, but the series that ran from 1957 to 1966. Predictably into the courtroom by the thirty-first minute of each show, L.A. attorney Mason proved that lawyers and justice can co-exist on the same planet by both (1) winning all his cases and (2) always trapping the real murderer who would, driven to un-

[8]Herbert London, "What TV Drama Is Teaching Our Children," *The New York Times,* August 23, 1987.

bearable guilt by Perry's accusation, blurt out a confession in a packed courtroom before a police officer could break through the crowd to Mirandize her.

The show features, in addition to square-philanthropist Raymond Burr as Perry, William Hopper as television's most wholesome detective, Paul Drake; and William Talman as history's best loser, District Attorney Hamilton Burger, who frequently joined Perry and Della (Barbara Hale) for lunch after the trial for a healthy helping of crow.

Square Villains! The Rogues. This family of international smooth talkers, featuring debonair squares Charles Boyer, David Niven, and Gig Young, would play their confidence games only on behalf of a good cause. Like a charity benefit, or more likely to help good-hearted simpletons who lost their life's savings to the shrewd and immoral kind of confidence trickster.

Square Sitcom: Ozzie and Harriet. The Nelsons, a slower-paced family show from the fifties, with no drugs (although the characters, by comparison with today's sitcom stars, seem to be tranquilized with Miltown), sex, heavy conversation, or questionable girlfriends for well-scrubbed future rocker Ricky and older brother David. A typical moment of dramatic tension: Harriet needs the car to go to the store, but Ozzie hasn't returned from the soda fountain yet.

Square Fun: Mr. Rogers. A calming break from the urban hubbub of Sesame Street, Mr. Rogers' neighborhood is terribly soothing for stressed-out adults as well. Unlike the Saturday morning kid shows sponsored by toymakers as cartoon showcases for their expensive products, Fred Rogers believes that the proper toys are milk cartons, paper towel tubes, and other simple objects requiring imagination, "the best plaything of all."

Square "Moonlighting": The Thin Man. Don't miss this series of classic films with William Powell and Myrna Loy as private detectives Nick and Nora Charles who, with clever-pet-trick originator Asta, the dog, drink martinis and engage in the snappiest dialogue ever to pass the properly strict censorship of the 1930s.

The Rogues. No moral morons in this family of crooks.

The Nelsons. Nothing serious to worry about, ever.

Mr. Rogers' Neighborhood. Yuppie Puppies need not apply.

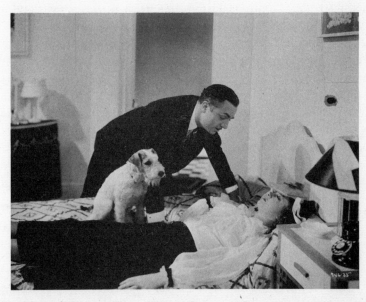

Nick and Asta comfort Nora after one dry martini too many.

*P*EAK *E*XPERIENCES

Into every square life, some excitement must fall (but not too much). Other than strictly marital sex, you might wonder what could quicken the pulse of a responsible adult who must be ever-vigilant, serious, essentially negative on the subject of fun, and watchful of others' excesses. Approved sources of exhilaration are as follows:

Sound Investments for the Nineties

Nothing gives adults a shimmer of satisfaction that runs from heart to extremities like the realization that their investments will remain safe and sound throughout practically any global event and economic debacle.

High Risk. If you have an appetite for high anxiety, you may choose such maximum-risk investments as utilities, rails and industrials, or savings accounts insured to the maximum $100,000 by the Federal Deposit Insurance Corporation. However, a more prudent portfolio strategy seems better advised for the turbulent years ahead.

Low Risk. Highly recommended are stocks of canned food and buried gold in your backyard to protect your family's downside risk of not surviving war, famine, rioting, and natural disasters such as the fast-approaching New Ice Age (feel the chill already?). However, the three "sleeper" investments for the next decade promise to be those that take full advantage of our hopelessly perplexing new tax laws.

1. *Buy a cruise ship as your second home,* which will surely qualify as a pleasure boat and provide you an incremental income when you fill all 367 cabins with paying guests as well.

2. *Lease clothing to employees owned by corporations.* Since employee leasing never caught on in the eighties, the innovation of the nineties will be ownership of employees by the companies they work for, as employees bargain their souls for a lifetime

of security. Stock up on business suits to lease out on a 12-, 24- or 36-month basis (no down payment) as a fully deductible "office supply" for purchased individuals, who need clothes as surely as a desk needs paper clips!

3. *Sell shares in fallout shelters.* Why did time sharing earn a bad reputation in the eighties? Because the properties were solely for the pursuit of pleasure, thus were morally indefensible. In the nineties everybody will want a fallout shelter, but they'll be in short supply. The solution: share the risk! And since everybody will probably want to use them at the same time, stock up on canned canapés! There's always room for one more.

Reliving the Glorious Past in Musicals

Chances are, if you came of age in the seventies or eighties, you think musicals were always like *Evita* and *Cats*. What a tradition you missed! Wait until you experience the real musicals from the Golden Age of Broadway, which will undoubtedly be revived for the Restoration Era. Run, don't walk down memory lane to your nearest collectible records store and pick up these immortal albums for a taste of musical perfection:

1. Ethel Merman in anything. Best Bet: *Happy Hunting.*

2. Jackie Gleason in *Take Me Along,* featuring the Great One's ode to drinking too much, "Little Green Snake," and Walter Pidgeon belting out a bittersweet "I'm Staying Young."

3. Judy Holliday in *Bells Are Ringing,* with Jean Stapleton (later Edith Bunker of "All in the Family") as her sidekick. Best song: "The Party's Over." It's time to call it a day. Hear it and weep.

4. Julie Andrews in *The Sound of Music,* the stirring saga of the Trapp family's escape to America to fulfill their lifelong dream of running a ski lodge for New Yorkers. Includes the choice coming-of-age song for perfectly square teenagers, "When You're Sixteen Going on Seventeen."

5. Richard Burton in *Camelot*. Contrary to popular belief, this was a musical before it became a Presidential administration in 1960. Burton artfully brings down the castle with the pre-feminist "How to Handle a Woman."

Ethel Merman frightens the horses in **Happy Hunting.**

Julie Andrews tells the children why they should want to buy the world a Coke in **The Sound of Music.**

Homes Away from Home: Square Valhallas

Where you decide to go on vacation and recharge your batteries
will affect your responsible performance all year long. Choose
your destination well to ensure that a good time will be had by
all, and that you can in good conscience send postcards to family
and friends that say "having a wonderful time, wish you were
here."

Don't Drink the Bourbon: Hazards of Foreign Travel

The whole point of careful vacation planning, like joining the
right country club, is to minimize your risk of encountering the
unfamiliar and even vaguely threatening.

Consider this sad but typical case of a foreign "dream" vacation
that became a nightmare:[9]

> *In 1977 thirty-two Coventry housewives decided to
> "pop over to Paris" for the weekend. Such were the
> delays and disasters encountered that they arrived in
> the French capital with only two hours to spare before
> they were due to return home.*
>
> *After eight hours on the boat and fifteen hours on
> the coach, the housewives got out to find that they were
> still eighty miles from Paris. They booked into a hotel
> at Compiègne where they had to rest three to a room.
> "Then a cat wet the bed," said one of the women, "and
> we were six to a room."*
>
> *When they eventually got to Paris, they found that
> the courier couldn't speak French. After a quick look
> around, they set off for home. They called at the same
> hotel where the same cat wet the bed again and also
> ate their chicken lunch prior to their arrival.*

Suitable caution will eliminate from your itinerary all foreign
shores, with three notable exceptions:

[9]Stephen Pile, *Heroic Failures* (New York: Ballantine, 1979), p. 38.

Scotland, Preferably in Winter

The probable origin of all things square in the U.S.A. is this bleak yet uplifting land of tartan plaids, scotch whiskey, the St. Andrew's Golf Course, and Harris tweed.

When planning your trip to Scotland, make sure you include these must-sees:

- *Highland Games.* After being whipped into a frenzy by bagpipe playing, hefty Scottish youths wearing the colorful kilts of their clans "toss the caber," a log actually longer than one and a half Cadillacs, which must be hurled by one individual without wearing a truss.

- *Scottish Agricultural Museum.* Near Edinburgh, the Museum features reminders of Scotland's character-building heritage of hard labor, such as the Shetland spade, sickle, and scythe. Watch your fingers.

- *Castle Fisheries.* This authentic fish farm near Inveraray instructs visitors in the fish-rearing practices necessary to bring a rainbow trout to man- or womanhood. A visit to the "sick tank" will remind you how lucky you are to be both well and human.

Canada's Maritime Provinces

If you can't make it to Scotland, the next-best thing is right in your own backyard: the Maritime Provinces of Nova Scotia (New Scotland), New Brunswick, and Prince Edward Island. Winters are blissfully harsh along their craggy coasts, chilled by the Labrador Current. Be sure to visit:

- *Alexander Graham Bell's summer home,* located in the village of Baddeck in Nova Scotia, which features no second-class phones.

- *Prince Edward Island,* where there is absolutely nothing to do but remark on the redness of the soil.

- *A side trip to Newfoundland.* Make the settlements of

Useless Bay and Witless Bay your destinations on this wild, rocky island. The "Newfies" are a colorful lot, whose conversation will delight you with quaint expressions, such as:[10]

> *"I have a noggin to scrape"*
> *(a hard task to perform).*
>
> *"She's all mops and brooms"*
> *(has untidy hair).*
>
> *"Long may your big jib draw"*
> *(good luck).*

Bleak House. *Visit Scotland in winter, and you'll build character while others idly soak up the sun.*

[10]*Michelin Tourist Guide to Canada* (Québec: Michelin Tires, Canada, Ltd., 1987), pp. 198–205.

No-Thrills on a Budget. *A tour of Canada's Maritime Provinces captures the crisp flavor of Scotland closer to home.*

Inside the Bermuda Square

For the balmy Good Life, Square-style, come to Bermuda, the resort island where you can still find authentic pillories for humiliating adulterers, horse-drawn carriages in place of the familiar rental cars, and houses with Christian names instead of numbers! It's the only island resort, in fact, where the locals wear tartans and Harris tweeds in winter.

As you enjoy the restful charms of Bermuda, you'll want to bring home memories of:

■ The unfinished cathedral (Hamilton) for open-air prayer.

■ The Gombey Dancers who appear on Boxing Day (December

26), not to be confused with the Jamaican "Gumby" dancers who dress like large green erasers.

▪ The only Square tropical wear, Bermuda shorts, which may be worn with a dinner jacket when you're invited to a reception at the Governor's.

Square Nirvana: *Bermuda, the only New Establishment Resort under the sun.*

Beat the Crowds

The insider vacation spots for the nineties, though, are right here
in the U.S.A. Whether you relish the everlasting quiet of a petrified forest or the authentic good cheer of an early American
settlement, you'll keep the dollar at home while you broaden your
horizons.

▪ Fort Hood's open military base in Killeen, Texas, is the
largest in the (free) world, with guided tours and two
breathtaking military museums.

▪ The Petrified Forest National Park near Holbrook, Arizona,
provides plenty of shade during the summer, and an opportunity to see your problems in perspective against the
fossilized backdrop of a 200-million-year-old forest.

▪ Holland, Michigan, is Tulip Capital of the U.S.A., and home
of America's squarest soft drink, "Squirt."

▪ Old Sturbridge Village, Massachusetts, will help you locate
your roots with a taste of American life c. 1820. Genuine
sheep graze on the village green, and period church services
go easy on the fire and brimstone. At the Publick House
Inn, you can sample fried mush, roasted chestnuts, codfish
cakes, and sticky buns before you head up the crooked and
creaking stairs to your Restoration Era room.

▪ Delray (Dull-ray) Beach, Florida. While the hip flock to
Miami's South Beach and Key West, you can sit perfectly
still in this New Establishment community near Palm Beach.

▪ Lucy the Elephant in Margate, New Jersey, is a former
hotel built in the shape of a mastodon. Stand on her back
65 feet in the sky for a stunning view of New Jersey.[11]

▪ The World's longest Breakfast Table, in Battle Creek, Michigan (Breakfast Capital of the World), serves a hearty
breakfast four blocks long, courtesy of Kellogg's, General
Foods, and Ralston-Purina.[12]

[11]*Birnbaum's United States,* 1987 (Boston: Houghton Mifflin, 1986), p. 801.
[12]*Ibid.,* p. 804.

The Petrified Forest. *No living things to disturb your tranquillity.*

Tulip time in Holland, Michigan. *A vacation for puttering around the motel.*

Old Sturbridge Village. *The way we were, without the Indian attacks and diphtheria.*

LIVING THROUGH THE KIDS

Now that we must bid a fond farewell, a thought on the greatest satisfaction of all: living your own life over, vicariously, through your children.

While you had to spend half your life a hip trendy, your little ones may have the advantage of growing up perfectly Square from Day One. Little Chip, Susie, and Biff need never experience the agonies you suffered of wondering what to wear, dealing with the chronic tension of a Sexual Revolution, experiencing a life of precarious luxury on high-risk investments, watching MTV. Teach your children well. Watch their square roots like little acorns grow. And, chances are, they'll stay with you for a long, long time.

As Dorothy pointed out, there's no place like home for the square child.

The Ancestral Condominium. *Living at home and loving it after twenty-one (but we still can't get that old hipster Dad to church).*

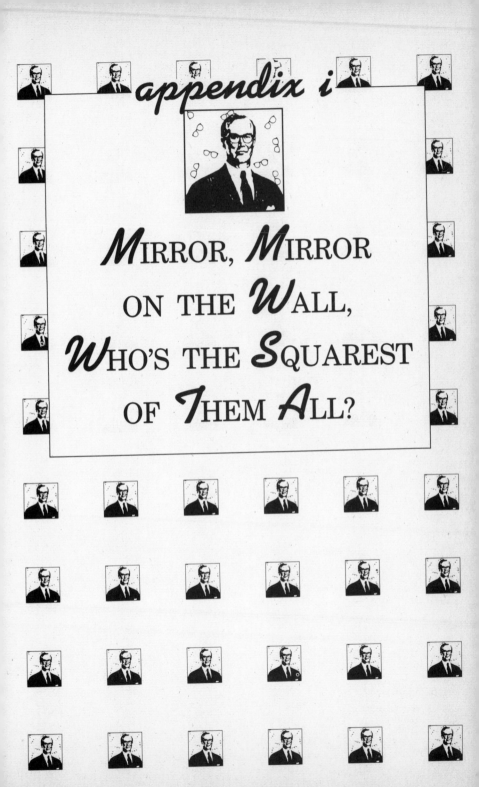

appendix i

Mirror, Mirror on the Wall, Who's the Squarest of Them All?

Born Square

■ ■ ■ ■ ■

WILLIAM F. BUCKLEY, JR.
Establishment Spokesperson Since the 1950s

MICHAEL J. FOX
Played Little Adult Alex Keaton

> Quote: *"I would gladly dance on the grave of Yuppie-dom and greed any day."*
>
> *Interview*, 1988

TED KOPPEL
TV Journalist with Visible Values

> *Quote:* "*What Moses brought down from the mountain top were not the Ten Suggestions.*"
>
> *Time,* 1987

Dared to Be Squared

■ ■ ■ ■ ■ ■

BILL COSBY

Then

Hip Comic

Now

#1 Adult

DAN AYKROYD

Then

Blues Brother

Now

Sergeant Friday

GRACE SLICK

Then

Druggie Singer

Now

Drug-free Singer

JERRY RUBIN

Then	***Then***
Yippie	Yuppie

Now

Square

PETER PAN

Then

Middle-aged Children's Agitator

Now

Middle-aged Scout Leader

appendix ii

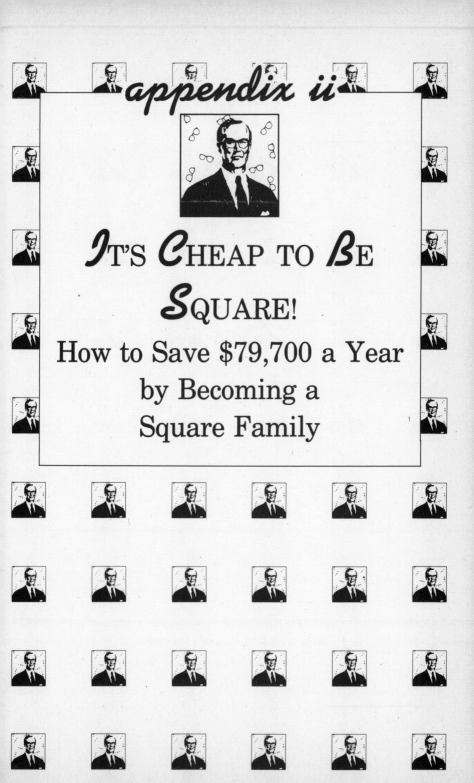

It's Cheap to Be Square!

How to Save $79,700 a Year by Becoming a Square Family

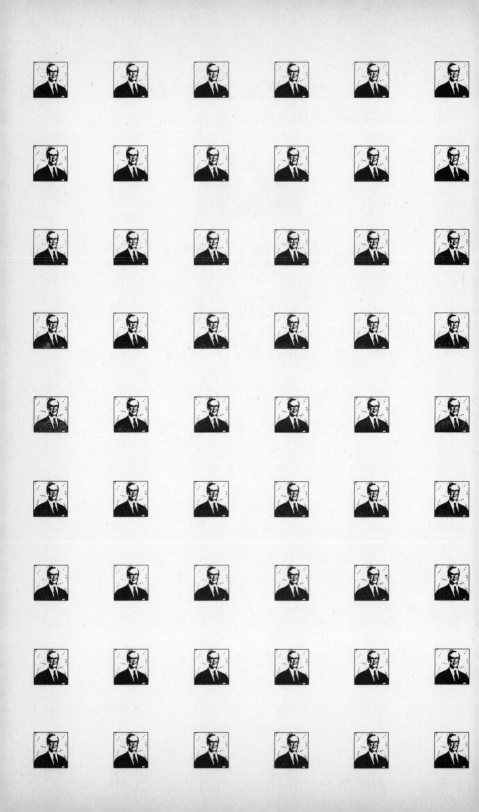

■ ■ ■ ■ ■ ■

Yuppie Family 1990 Budget		Square Family 1990 Budget	
Housing: Condo with view in Chicago	$36,000	**Housing:** Colonial in Louisville, KY	$12,000
Car: 1990 Saab Turbo Convertible	$ 7,200	**Car:** 1958 T-Bird	$ 1,200
1990 Volvo Station Wagon	$ 4,800	1958 Country Squire Wagon	$ 1,200
Insurance: $500,000 term	$ 3,000	**Insurance:** $150,000 whole life	$ 1,200
Food: Trendy restaurants and nouvelle cuisine at home	$15,000	**Food:** Simple fare	$ 3,600
Entertainment: Movies, new video games and compact discs	$18,000	Reading, puttering, lawn games	$ 1,200
Clothing: Designer, seasonal	$12,000	**Clothing:** Functional, all-weather, (never out of style)	$ 2,000
Charitable: Yuppie PAC	$ 100	United Way, church	$ 6,000
	$108,000		$28,400
		YOU SAVE:	$79,700

■ ■ ■ ■ ■ ■